DIPLOMA MILLS

DIPLOMA MILLS
Degrees of Fraud

David W. Stewart
Henry A. Spille

AMERICAN COUNCIL **ᗘᗙ** MACMILLAN
ON EDUCATION PUBLISHING COMPANY
NEW YORK

Collier Macmillan Publishers
LONDON

Copyright © 1988 by American Council on Education and
Macmillan Publishing Company
A Division of Macmillan, Inc.

Macmillan Publishing Company
866 Third Avenue, New York, N.Y. 10022

Collier Macmillan Canada, Inc.

Library of Congress Catalog Card Number: 88-17462

Printed in the United States of America

printing number
1 2 3 4 5 6 7 8 9 10

Library of Congress Cataloging in Publication Data

Stewart, David Wood, 1929–
    Diploma mills: degrees of fraud / David W. Stewart, Henry A. Spille.
        p.   cm. -- (The American Council on Education/Macmillan series on higher
education)
    ISBN 0-02-930410-5
    1. Diploma mills—United States.   2. Universities and colleges—
United States—Corrupt practices.   I. Spille, Henry A.   II. Title.
III. Series.
LB2388.S74 1988   88-17462
378'2—dc19   CIP

CONTENTS

Foreword

FRED M. HECHINGER
The New York Times

Early in the 1960s, I reported in *The New York Times* that annually thousands of fraudulent degrees were being sold by diploma mills to a clientele of chiselers and dupes at a cost of hundreds of thousands, perhaps even millions, of dollars. More than twenty-five years later, little has changed, except the price for degrees which, like that for all other commodities, is considerably higher. Phony medical degrees may fetch as much as $35,000, cheap considering the returns to be expected from such an investment.

Why has there been no change for the better despite periodic exposure of this costly and dangerous racket? Why is it still possible for a five-year-old to become a "Nutrition Consultant" to expose the fraudulent trade? Part of the answer lies between the lines of this extraordinarily valuable book: no insurers could be found to protect any publisher of the volume against possible court challenges if the authors had persisted in their original plan of including an actual listing of diploma mills. No matter that they are highly respected and responsible researchers, their plan simply proved too hot for insurance companies and lawyers to handle.

Diploma mills are a hot item, indeed. They are not engaging, as the authors make clear, in victimless crime. Their victims are many: customers, many of them foreigners, ignorant of American higher education's legitimate requirements; employers who put their trust in worthless, though often elaborate, documents masquerading as credentials; consumers, including patients, who pay for falsely credentialed services; and perhaps most regrettable, legitimate but non-

traditional educational institutions who are mistaken for diploma mills operating deliberately under similar titles and
logos.

Having found it impossible to expose fraudulent degree-
granting "institutions"—many of them consisting of little more
than a Post Office box—in an actual directory listing, the
authors provide the next best consumer protection and spur
for more effective policing and law enforcement: a thorough
study of what diploma mills look like and how they ply their
trade. They have prepared an essential guide for anyone who
wants to learn how to distinguish legitimate from fraudulent
degree-granting institutions. They have provided a guide for
employers or potential customers to protect themselves against
fraud; and, one may hope, for law enforcement agencies to
take action against those who hold and, more important, those
who provide the deceptive pieces of paper.

The ultimate challenge of this long overdue book ought
to be to the states which must agree on uniform legislation
to make it possible to prosecute and shut down diploma mills
anywhere in the United States. Unless such action is taken,
the shadowy operations, which rarely own any real estate,
will continue to move from states which take legal action
against them to those which tolerate fraud and deception.

History has shown that diploma mills are a hardy weed.
This book serves two purposes: in its cautions on how to avoid
poison mushrooms, it makes the current scene less hazardous;
in its recommendations for change, it points the way to getting
rid of the dangerous weed altogether.

Preface

The six-year-long effort culminating in this volume did not begin with an intention to write a book about diploma mills. The original objective was to gather information about what was initially perceived as a rather insignificant, if entertaining, problem that threatened the integrity of college degrees. As it became evident that the problem was anything but small and that we had a bear by the tail, our intentions became more focused.

This volume about the diploma mill industry is written to assist readers in identifying organizations that call themselves colleges or universities but that are not, in any true sense, colleges or universities. In addition to prospective students, this information may be of particular interest to college and university registrars and other administrators, employers in both the private and public sectors, military personnel and education officers, state government officials, higher education association executives, and foreign nationals who are unfamiliar with the American system of higher education.

Diploma Mills: Degrees of Fraud has been produced under guidelines approved by the American Council on Education (ACE) Commission on Educational Credit and Credentials. This body and the Council's Board of Directors have authorized development of this volume as a statement in defense of the integrity of educational credit and credentials as these measures of academic achievement are generally understood and accepted within the American higher education community. It is clear that ACE with its membership of college, university, and higher education association chief executive officers is the logical national organization to undertake this task.

In this volume, we have endeavored to be as specific about various aspects of the problem of ersatz colleges and universities as is possible in the present litigious era. We define the problem as we see it and give dozens of examples of what we consider to be, at best, questionable activity going by the label of higher education. We name the names of persons convicted of crimes associated with diploma mill and accreditation mill operations. We tell how one can identify a diploma mill in both its legal and illegal forms. The relationship of diploma mills to fraudulent occupational licensure is described, and academic credit and degrees—the legitimate variety—are defined. How the roles of state and federal government entities and accrediting agencies interplay in controlling academic fraud is explained, and we identify states in which diploma mill activity is especially rampant. Legitimate programs of nontraditional higher education are sorted out from not-so-legitimate programs. Foreign diploma mills in America and American diploma mills operating overseas are exposed. We describe and analyze the trade in phony transcripts, letters of reference, educational or career counseling, honorary doctorates, false certification, dissertations and term papers, misleading directories—even class rings and jewelry. The concluding chapter contains recommendations for reversing the diploma mill boom in America.

In a fully packed appendix we have supplied supplemental resources that should be useful to anyone in need of further information. This material includes a list of important names and addresses, a selected bibliography, and capsule summaries of laws governing educational institutions in every state.

Special ethical hazards attend any effort to expose shoddy or illegal activities in any field. We believe that our responsibility to supply the unvarnished truth to the public is matched by a responsibility to be absolutely accurate and fair in our portrayal of activities that we believe to be less than what should be expected of any American college or university. We hope that readers of this volume will find that we have been faithful to our intentions.

David W. Stewart
Henry A. Spille
Washington, D.C.

Acknowledgments

We could not have produced a book about a problem so dispersed, so covert, so complicated, and so sensitive without the help of many people who were willing to share their knowledge and expertise with us. We want to acknowledge this assistance.

Crucial support at the outset of this project was provided by Jerry W. Miller, formerly Vice President for Academic Affairs and Institutional Relations at the American Council on Education (now President of the Association of Independent Colleges and Schools). Comparable support was received in full measure from Elbert W. Ockerman and Verne A. Duncan, former Chairmen of ACE's Commission on Educational Credit and Credentials. Robert H. Atwell, ACE's President, was an assertive proponent of the project when it was discussed by the ACE Board. Each of them, while fully aware of the hazards and risks, saw beyond these to larger questions of need and possibilities.

Authors of a book are lucky if they have a knowledgeable, fair, and persistent critic who challenges their approaches in constructive ways. We had such an asset in the person of Richard M. Millard, former President (now retired) of the Council on Postsecondary Accreditation (COPA). As the chief national spokesperson for generally recognized accrediting agencies in the United States, it would have been easy for Dr. Millard to urge us to take a very hard line in our criticisms of accrediting entities that are not in the COPA family. Instead, he was a forceful voice for fairness and integrity as we dealt with difficult questions associated with the sponsorship of accreditation. Richard Millard possesses a strong sense of professional ethics which was an inspiration to us and which we hope is reflected in every sentence of this account of unethical behavior in the world of higher education.

It takes a long time to read a manuscript having fifteen chapters—especially one focusing on so complex a problem. All of these individuals took time that they could ill afford to read this volume and to help us with constructive criticism and comments: William H. Warren, Michael J. Pelczar, Jr., Jerry W. Miller, Warren D. Evans, Joyce A. Scott, James C. Votruba, Eugene J. Sullivan, William K. Haldeman, Sheldon E. Steinbach, Patricia A. Skinner, Billie L. Ackerman, Peter Meyer, Lee Porter, Frederick C. Kintzer, William J. MacLeod, David A. Longanecker, and Robert Carbone. One other person read the full manuscript and provided valuable corrections and commentary. For good reasons, he does not wish his name made public. He knows who he is, and we wish him to have at least this oblique evidence of our appreciation.

A number of people read and provided critiques on portions of the manuscript, and we wish to acknowledge their help. They are: Kay J. Andersen, Jonathan Brown, Barry L. Cobb, Otho Allen Ezell, John W. Griffin, Elbert W. Ockerman, F. P. Nater, Constance Odems, John H. Peterson, Peter Reinecke, Leslie N. Ross, Barbara Binker, C. Wayne Williams, Marianne Lettus, Alan S. Krech, Karl Haigler, Kenneth E. Young, and Michael Vorbeck.

The chapter on the state of California's contribution to the diploma mill problem is one of the most sensitive portions of this book and required diligent care and effort in research and writing. We want to thank all of the people who helped us with the essential task of acquiring an accurate information base. Chief among these individuals is Dr. John H. Peterson who recently retired as Director of California's Private Postsecondary Education Division of the State Department of Education. We also appreciate the assistance of other members of the Division staff, notably Morris L. Krear and Charles A. Manning. William K. Haldeman and Bruce D. Hamlett of the California Postsecondary Education Commission, Jonathan Brown of the Association of Independent California Colleges and Universities, and Kay J. Andersen of the Western Association of Schools and Colleges also provided valuable advice and commentary. Not everyone agrees with every aspect of our analysis of the problem, but any differences with us or each other were at all times expressed with full respect for the integrity of differing points of view.

Tracking the activities of American diploma mills in foreign countries is not easy if it has to be done only from this side of the ocean. Fortunately, we were able to obtain very excellent assistance from two European higher education officials who understand the problem well and want something done about it. Michael Vorbeck, Head of the Section for Educational Research and Documentation, Secretariat General, of the Council of Europe in Strasbourg, France, has provided much helpful information. Dr. G. Reuhl, Director of the Secretariat of the Conference of German Ministers of Education, Federal Republic of Germany, was also most helpful at a conference in Washington and later at a meeting he arranged with Mr. Vorbeck in Frankfort, West Germany.

We appreciate as well the splendid cooperation received from state government officials responsible for overseeing nonpublic, degree-granting institutions in each state. Because of them, we are able to present here a summary of relevant state laws, a valuable service in itself.

We want to thank our colleague and friend, Victoria Falco, who allowed us to use her name and home address in collecting information from suspected diploma mills and questionable accrediting agencies. Her skills as an actress (she really is one) were amply documented every time her telephone rang— as it frequently did after our letters of inquiry went out.

C.E. Floyd, Assistant Superintendent of the Federal Prison Camp at Maxwell Air Force Base in Montgomery, Alabama, granted permission for a convicted diploma mill operator who was an inmate at that institution to review and critique our manuscript. We appreciate this assistance which enabled us to obtain information that would not otherwise have been accessible.

Randy Willetts, Inspector with the U.S. Postal Inspection Service, provided photographs and related materials that helped bring the Caribbean medical school scandal into sharper focus. Our advice to would-be diploma mill operators is think twice before crossing him.

Jonathan D. Ezekiel provided valuable assistance by putting in the long hours necessary to review and categorize the information presented in the various diploma mill catalogs and promotional pieces. He also analyzed survey forms providing information as to state statutes governing the incorporation and authorization of higher education institutions.

James Murray made many essential contributions to this volume—and capped them by inventing the accurate and imaginative title.

Beatrice Wallace with her usual quiet competence organized production of the manuscript at several crucial points. We appreciate her work not just on this project but on all projects every day of the week. Adele Lassere came late to the project but quickly made herself an effective member of the production team. In so doing, she gave us an example of grace under pressure.

All of these individuals provided helpful information. Some of them saved us from what would have been embarrassing errors. However, remaining mistakes in this volume, if any, are those of the authors.

The American Council on Education

A NATIONAL MONITOR OF CREDENTIAL INTEGRITY

The American Council on Education (ACE) is the major voice in American higher education and serves as the locus for discussion and decision-making on higher education issues of national importance. An independent, nonprofit association founded in 1918, the Council membership includes presidents and chief executive officers of most accredited colleges and universities, as well as chief executive officers of national and regional higher education associations. ACE, located in Washington, D.C., strives to assist members in assuring quality education by providing leadership and guidance on issues of national, state, and local importance.

The Center for Adult Learning and Educational Credentials of ACE is the pioneer in establishing policies and procedures for awarding college credit to adults for learning attained outside the sponsorship of legally authorized and accredited postsecondary educational institutions. The Center began evaluating courses in 1945 for the military as a means of assisting thousands of veterans in their attempt to obtain college credit recommendations.

This system of evaluating formal courses offered by the armed services was extended to civilian organizations. The evaluations and credit recommendations now extend to courses sponsored by associations, business, government, industry, and unions, as well as learning acquired from work and life experiences, independent reading and study, and mass media. The Center's programs include Credit by Examination, Military Evaluations, the Program on Noncollegiate Sponsored Instruction, Registries, and General Educational Development (GED) Testing Service which enables people who have not graduated from high school to obtain an equivalency diploma.

DIPLOMA
MILLS

1

Welcome to Fast Lane U— And To Graduating Magna Cum Fraud

Fast Lane U—to the busy adult in search of an educational credential it sounds too good to be true. But the promise of a speedy degree *has* been confirmed in writing—and in a follow-up phone call from the university's Director of Admissions.

The program seems ideal. There are no entrance requirements, not even a bachelor's degree is necessary for admission to the graduate programs. Only the form for describing life experience presents a challenge, but that's worth the effort because it's likely to result in an award of credits totaling nearly three-fourths of the number needed for graduation. No conference with the admissions officer is necessary. The form is merely filled out and mailed.

After reviewing the completed life experience form, the admissions counselor states that the entire degree program can be finished in six months, maybe less. There is no nonsense about going to class either. Several telephone conversations with a faculty adviser plus a five-day "Intensive Seminar" at a nearby motel should be all that is necessary to earn that coveted piece of parchment.

The price is right, too—just $800 for a bachelor's degree. A master's degree (in any one of 45 subjects) comes a bit more dear at $1,250. At only $2,300, the Ph.D. is the real bargain, especially since it may qualify so many of its holders for a new position or a promotion or a salary increase in their present jobs.

To make everything perfect, all of this largess comes from a university that is perfectly legal. Isn't Fast Lane University officially listed as authorized to operate in public records for anyone who cares to check it out? Accreditation is no problem. Fast Lane has it from the Accrediting Commission of the American Association of Superific Colleges and Universities.

So much for appearances. But let's move a bit further into the ramshackle academic structure that lies behind the elegant facade. To be sure, Fast Lane University was "registered" in 1986 under a law that permitted anyone to start a college or university by simply submitting to state government officials a statement showing its location, administrators and board members, number of volumes in its library and accreditation (if any). Beyond that, about all that has been required is the filing of an annual update of this information.

The fact not mentioned in any of the university's literature is that these minimal state requirements have long been a national joke.

Accreditation was also a breeze for this organization. Fast Lane U is "fully accredited" by an entity that was organized, and is controlled, by Fast Lane's owners, among others. Left unstated is the fact that accreditation by this body is not recognized by the Council on Postsecondary Accreditation (COPA), the national organization that works to coordinate all nongovernmental accrediting activities conducted in the United States at the postsecondary level. On this account, Fast Lane's degrees and credits are not accepted by most American colleges and universities.

The academic program, such as it is, is conducted by faculty who generally hold Ph.D.s from Fast Lane University or similar organizations. Some faculty members listed do hold degrees from legitimate universities, but all of them are moonlighting at Fast Lane U. They are employed full-time in other jobs. Some do not even know their names are listed as faculty. The organization's physical facilities consist of two rooms in an office building located in a rundown shopping center. There is no library nor are there any arrangements under which non-owned library facilities may be used by Fast Lane students. And so on. Fast Lane University, while fictitious, typifies a newly aggressive breed of diploma mills on the American scene.

The American Council on Education (ACE), through its Center for Adult Learning and Educational Credentials, serves as an unofficial clearinghouse for information about questionable academic organizations. For six years, we have been keeping an informal log of calls, letters of inquiry, and news media stories, as well as collecting catalogs and related materials from suspected diploma mills, using several Maryland addresses. Following are capsule accounts of typical incidents and reports from ACE files which serve to outline the symptoms of the diploma mill problem and show how the system works.

• A housewife in New Jersey called to find out more about the Missouri-based university from which she was about to obtain a bachelor's degree. For three years she had been receiving lessons and assignments and completing them conscientiously. She had also been paying tuition promptly and with regularity. The university had changed its location several times during this period, and it had always been difficult to reach anyone by phone. Lately, she had become especially concerned since her envelopes were returned marked "Moved, Left No Forwarding Address." The institution's phone had also been disconnected.

• A sergeant-major in the Inspector General's office at a large military training base reported that a soldier under his supervision had submitted a diploma showing that he had earned an associate degree that would qualify him for promotion to warrant officer. Upon investigation, it was learned that the organization listed, a notorious diploma mill, had been closed many years previously after investigation by the FBI.

• An executive in the training department of a large manufacturing organization called to find out if she could safely recommend two universities domiciled in another state that were promoting in mailings to the firm's employees degrees that could ordinarily be completed by correspondence only, within six months. Both organizations operated legally but were organized under state statutes that had virtually no requirements bearing on institutional quality or degree integrity. Neither institution was accredited by an agency recognized by the Council on Postsecondary Accreditation (COPA). ACE files were replete with complaints about both institutions and reports of their questionable activities in the United States and in Europe.

• A government official reported that a high school classmate of his purchased a doctoral degree in psychology from a diploma mill. The purchaser then went to work for an airline, counseling employees for stress. She was in this job until someone reviewing her transcript recognized the name of the diploma mill.

• The registrar at a Canadian university called to inquire about the status of a university in California. A man holding a bachelor's degree from the California institution had been denied admission to the Canadian university's graduate program on grounds that his bachelor's degree was not acquired from an accredited university. In response, the man had submitted a letter from the chief academic officer of the California institution stating that under the most recent California statutes, his university has state "approval" that is "equivalent to accreditation."

• A representative of a group of Nigerian students called to find out why his group could not gain admission to any American graduate school even though they held bachelor's degrees from a university listing itself as "accredited" in its catalog. Unfortunately, such accreditation was not by an agency recognized by COPA, a relevant fact absent from all of the university's promotional materials.

• A representative of a U.S. Department of Defense security clearance office called to inquire about a Ph.D. degree listed by an applicant for a sensitive job at the Pentagon. The degree had been granted some years back by a diploma mill that had long since been out of business.

• An official of a large executive search organization called to inquire about the credentials listed by a client seeking employment at the highest level in an international corporation. The university from which he held a Ph.D. was authorized to operate in the state of California. The official was suspicious on this account and also because the dissertation copy the applicant had submitted was written in "Oxford English," even though the man spoke no English himself.

• A middle-management executive at an east coast firm called to inquire about the Ph.D. degree-by-mail offered by a university based in Missouri. A friend of his had just entered the program and was awarded life experience credit in an amount almost equal to the number of credits required for degree completion. The friend expected to receive his degree in just three months. The caller wondered whether the program was sound. If so, he wanted to enter the program himself, since he needed a Ph.D. if he was to qualify for job advancement. Also he believed he would be a good candidate for the program because he had completed all but the dissertation requirement for the Ph.D. at an Ivy League university twenty years ago. Surely he would not need to do much more to qualify for the degree on the basis of his successful performance on the job.

• A Canadian law firm called to inquire about the status of an institution cited in the resume of an "expert witness" in engineering being called to testify in an important trial. The man's Ph.D. in engineering was earned at an American university that does not have COPA recognized accreditation.

• According to a newspaper clipping, the doctoral degrees held by a school superintendent and his key assistant in an eastern state returned to haunt them when the operators of the Arizona-based "university" from which they had obtained their degrees signed a consent decree in a state court admitting that they had committed consumer fraud. The superintendent said he had learned of the availability of the Doctor of Arts in Education degree from a classified advertisement in the *New York Times*. Both men had been eligible for reimbursement for courses claimed and for additional salary because of attaining higher education levels. Claims that they had been the victims of diploma mill fraud seemed lame when the committee investigating the affair found them unable to produce doctoral theses.

• One Saudi Arabian student enrolled at an institution, currently operating legally in California, and began work on a bachelor's degree in mechanical engineering. He worked on his assignments, writing about a fifteen to twenty page essay on each subject. After a few months, he was told that the degree requirements had been fulfilled, and he received his diploma. He felt cheated after learning that his degree would not be accepted by any American graduate school in engineering to which he applied. Had he not been told in advance that the university granting the bachelor's degree was accredited? Indeed it was, but not by an accrediting agency recognized by COPA—a fatal flaw if one intends to impress graduate school admissions officers.

• A postal inspector wrote about a well-thought-out scheme under which a diploma mill (disguised as a church) advertised the availability of high school equivalency diplomas which could be obtained by individuals who pass the tests of General Educational Development (GED). The clients were mostly very unsophisticated persons who paid a $15 enrollment fee and a $12 fee for each GED preparatory book they ordered (actually an official practice test copyrighted by ACE). Only much later were these individuals informed that the state department of education, not the church, was the official sponsor of the GED program and awarded the GED credential.

Most of these accounts and events are outcroppings of a vast terrain of diploma mill activity. It is an unhappy fact that the activities of such organizations are extensive in scope though they are often cleverly concealed. Employers and the public are being bilked. Naive or unscrupulous individuals are acquiring credentials that they do not earn and do not deserve; credentials that do not represent educational accomplishment. Certainly, the value of a degree from legitimate American colleges and universities is being undermined. The situation is a cause for concern on the part of anyone who cares about the future of American higher education.

2
What's The Problem?

Great care should be exercised before any organization is labeled as a diploma mill. Almost all innovative and nontraditional education, whatever its academic merit, may be carelessly denigrated as diploma mill activity by some educators. Such charges may be unfounded and based upon ignorance or erroneous interpretation of the philosophy and structure of the organization or program in question.

It must be acknowledged as well that even among traditional educators there is disagreement in defining degrees that can be awarded appropriately by academic institutions. Also, accredited institutions have been known to let standards lapse, and accrediting agencies may perform with something less than perfection in every instance. The American higher education community cannot be smug to the point of overlooking its own shortcomings.

Taking into account the appropriate caveats, what is a diploma mill? Basically a diploma mill is a person or an organization selling degrees or awarding degrees without an appropriate academic base and without requiring a sufficient degree of postsecondary-level academic achievement. The diplomas may bear the name of the issuing organization itself or may be fraudulent reproductions of diplomas awarded by legitimate colleges or universities. Diploma mills may operate either legally or illegally under state and federal laws.

What is an "appropriate academic base" as specified in the foregoing definition? There is no precise formula; colleges and universities can assume a variety of sizes and shapes and still qualify as real colleges and universities. But at the core of all such institutions must be an academic and financial resource base that is substantive enough to enable the institution to fulfill its mission.

At an institution providing instruction in the traditional manner, the faculty should, of course, have academic credentials appropriate for teaching the subject matter and evaluating the acquisition of learning. The curriculum should reflect sound planning by persons who are thoroughly familiar with the content of the subject matters. There should be an adequate library or learning resource center, or arrangements should be in place for students to use other appropriate library facilities. Instructional support services (e.g., academic advising) and computer services also need to be in place. Academic records should be developed, maintained, and stored under appropriate academic protocols. The financial base should be sufficient to enable the institution to pay its employees and acquire resources necessary to provide effective instruction.

Again with reference to the definition of a diploma mill, what is a "sufficient degree of postsecondary-level academic achievement"? This means that an institution should do more than collect money, grade a few papers, and issue a diploma. Course requirements should specify achievement at the postsecondary education level and assessment procedures should be in place to determine whether students have indeed acquired skills or knowledge beyond those required for high school graduation and at a level consistent with the degrees being sought.

If the institution is nontraditional in that it offers external degrees or does not itself offer instruction, adequate procedures should be in place to assure that students have attained college-level learning under the sponsorship of other institutions and organizations. (A full description of the threat posed by diploma mills to sound programs of nontraditional postsecondary education appears in chapter 5 of this volume.)

Diploma mills come in several varieties. In its simplest form, the diploma mill has few academic pretensions. It simply sells a diploma or degree to a person upon payment of a fee and does not require demonstration of the achievement of college-level learning. Such diplomas may carry the name of the diploma mill itself, or they may be duplicates of diplomas issued by legitimate colleges and universities. Forged diplomas for several hundred fully accredited American colleges and universities were seized in the offices of a "mail order house" closed in 1984 by the FBI (Pence, 1984). Bogus transcripts and letters of recommendation may also be part of the wares offered by the diploma mill in its most pristine form.

These days more common than the pure diploma factory—and certainly constituting a clearer threat to the integrity of credit and credentials—is the diploma mill that will grant a degree while posing requirements that emulate but are far less demanding than those ordinarily specified at legitimate colleges and universities. These marginal organizations often thrive by advertising themselves as offering programs tailored to meet the unique needs of adult learners. Their promotional literature cites the inadequacy (often real enough) of many main-line higher education institutions in developing programs that are truly designed for adults.

Some diploma mills in the latter category are blatantly exploitive commercial enterprises run by people who have no regard for academic values. On the other hand, some questionable organizations are headed by individuals who are honest and well-intentioned but who do not have the background, resources, or competence necessary to organize and administer an institution awarding postsecondary-level degrees. The basic program may be respectable enough in its outlines, but instruction is likely to be thin at best and academically unsound.

What is causing the boom in diploma mill operation? The

U.S. House of Representatives Select Committee on Aging, in its 1985 analysis of the dimensions of the diploma mill problem, began by noting that the American public has sharply increased its level of educational attainment as measured by years in school. In 1940, the median number of school years completed by Americans was 8.6. By 1983, the same median figure had jumped to 12.3 according to the Committee report.

Postsecondary education accounts for the lion's share of the increase in education levels for Americans. The percentage of Americans completing four or more years at public and private colleges shot up from 7.7 percent in 1960 to nearly 20 percent in 1985.

In 1961–1962, approximately 383,000 legitimate bachelor's degrees and 38,000 first professional degrees were awarded to Americans, along with 85,000 master's and 12,000 doctoral degrees. In 1987–1988, it is projected that legitimate institutions will award approximately 465,000 associate degrees, 927,000 bachelor's degrees, 70,000 first professional degrees, 291,000 master's degrees, and 33,000 doctoral degrees.

The nation's credential consciousness begins, however, at the secondary education level. In 1984, results of a nationwide survey, designed to determine the role of educational credentials in the employment practices of companies and institutions in the private sector, were released by ACE's Center for Adult Learning and Educational Credentials. The study was cosponsored by ACE, the American Society for Training and Development (ASTD), and the American Society for Personnel Administration (ASPA). Fifteen hundred members of ASPA were asked to indicate their company's emphasis on educational credentials in its employment practices and to rate the importance of various skills and attitudes for employees in jobs that did not require more than a high school diploma or equivalency credential.

Employers reported placing considerable emphasis on educational credentials. About one-fourth of the companies had no jobs for adults with less than a high school diploma or equivalency credential. At approximately half of the companies, persons hired with less than a high school diploma could enhance their opportunities for promotion by obtaining a high school equivalency credential (Malizio and Whitney, 1985).

Holders of college and university degrees today find themselves in a very competitive job market. Many more occupations and professions are available only to those holding college or university degrees. Many jobs, too, have been upgraded, their specifications expanded to require higher levels of preparation.

The chart shows that salaries become progressively higher for persons holding advanced degrees (U.S. Congress, House, 11 December 1985, p. 125). In business, for example, a person holding a master's degree (M.B.A.) is offered on the average a salary of $26,580, whereas a person holding a baccalaureate degree receives an average offer of only $17,892, a difference of 49 percent. The same salary differential holds for civil engineers and chemists.

AVERAGE SALARY OFFERS TO DEGREE CANDIDATES (1983)

	Bachelor's	Master's	Doctoral
Accounting	$18,780	$22,692	—
Business	$17,892	$26,580	—
Chemistry	$20,544	$26,436	$32,328
Civil Engineering	$22,428	$27,120	$35,232
Humanities	$16,560	$19,404	—
Marketing	$16,932	$25,464	—
Mechanical Engineering	$25,152	$28,800	$37,800
Social Sciences	$15,840	$19,272	—

Given these pressures, it is small wonder that the nation is experiencing an explosive growth in diploma mills and related organizations. According to estimates prepared for the House of Representatives Select Committee on Aging in December of 1985, there may be upwards of 500,000 working Americans, or one out of every 200, who have secured jobs based on fraudulent credentials. Included in this estimate are 10,000 doctors (one in every fifty physicians) who are practicing with fraudulent or questionable credentials. In addition, more than 30 million, or one out of every three working Americans, may be employed based on credentials that have been altered in some way. (U.S. Congress, House, 11 December 1985, p. 123).

Who are the clients of American diploma mills? Answer: a wide range of people holding or aspiring to hold white-collar jobs who find themselves unable or unwilling to compete legitimately within an increasingly credential-conscious society. Some are extremely sophisticated and know full well that they are engaging in academic fraud. Others become diploma mill victims out of ignorance or naivete. Foreign citizens are prominent in both groups.

Anthony Geruntino, whose diploma mill enterprise was shattered by the FBI, reported that about 50 percent of his clients were interested in degrees at the baccalaureate level, 30 percent at the master's level, and 20 percent wanted a Ph.D. The age range was 25 to 65. Approximately nine out of ten clients were male. Business administration was the occupation of first choice, followed by engineering, the health professions, and teaching. Geruntino said he did not offer any degree in medicine because he felt such action would be "unconscionable" (U.S. Congress, House, 11 December 1985, p. 51). (For a full account of FBI investigations of diploma mills, see chapter 6.)

Among other clearly fraudulent degree holders reported by the FBI were a diplomat, an advertising executive, a savings and loan company executive, a college administrator, a school principal, hospital and bank supervisors, a well-known professional football player, and a U.S. Army chaplain.

As unlikely as it may seem, the military services have had their share of difficulties with personnel holding diploma mill degrees. After criticism resulting from public disclosure of fraudulent credentials possessed by a physician, the Army conducted an audit of all of its active duty and civilian physicians to verify their credentials. In testimony before the Subcommittee on Health and Long-Term Care of the House Select Committee on Aging, Brig. Gen. Thomas M. Geer stated that the Army was now requiring that the validity of each document submitted by its physicians be verified, "either telephonically or in writing, with the applicable educational training or licensing organization prior to employment or entrance on active duty" (U.S. Congress, House, 7 December 1984, p. 86).

Major Areas of Activity

The career/occupational/professional "hot spots" for diploma mill activity are relatively easy to pinpoint. One need only identify those subject areas where the demand for legitimate degrees is also quite heavy. A review of catalogs and other literature from extremely questionable organizations reveals that at the moment these topical clusters are the focus of especially heavy diploma mill activity: (1) business, (2) counseling and therapy, (3) medicine and health, (4) nutrition, (5) education, and (6) religion.

Business. The credentials presented by a prominent East Coast investment adviser were impressive; they included degrees from three very well-known institutions. In fact, however, he had none of the baccalaureate or master's degrees he claimed, though he did have falsified diplomas. This case is perhaps typical of the rising traffic in diploma mill degrees in business. In business and industry, it is common practice to base decisions about employment and promotion in part upon an individual's educational credentials, making the M.B.A. degree especially valuable to its holders.

Counseling. In many states, statutes governing the licensure of counselors or therapists are vague or nonexistent. In some jurisdictions psychotherapy, marriage counseling, and sexual therapy, for example, may be offered by almost anyone who hangs out a shingle (Association for Continuing Higher Education, September 1977, p. 25). This situation poses a golden opportunity for the practitioner who earns a diploma mill degree.

For example, marital and other personal counseling were the stock in trade of a therapist practicing in one southern state. His qualifications for this work included a baccalaureate and a master's degree in social work and a doctoral degree in developmental science. He was certified by the state as a clinical social worker. This man, however, had not acquired his degrees in quite the same way as most other practitioners in his city. He obtained them all from now-defunct diploma mills. He was nonetheless certified by the state to charge professional fees in counseling distressed clients, although he had no legitimate qualifications. Unfortunately, in the state in question, this case is not all that unusual. Furthermore, according to the FBI, holders of such diplomas also work as doctors, counselors, law enforcement officers, and prison guards (Fischer, 1985).

Health Sciences. While the most dramatic examples of diploma mill activity in the practice of medicine are high-lighted in reports issued by the 1984 U.S. House of Representatives Select Committee on Aging, fraud and deception in diplomas issued in related health sciences are more common. For example, in a western state, a health education center was founded by a person having a degree in "holistic health science" from an unaccredited university. In applying for a state grant of funds (which it eventually received), the center carefully avoided referring to its services as "treatment" or "therapy." Once the grant was received, however, the center is reported to have attracted unaware patients by using the term "therapies" or "treatments" in reference to services (Gray, 1985).

Nutrition. The field of nutrition is especially fertile as an arena for diploma mill and related fraud. In 1980, for example, one mass-market publication carried an article promoting a type of "megavitamin therapy" which recommended massive doses of possibly harmful products. A number of advertisements for products mentioned in the article appeared in subsequent issues. The article's author, a "nutrition researcher" and "biochemist," held a diploma mill Ph.D. (Herbert, 1982, p. 244).

In the same year, another publication ran an article about "diet myths" by a "nutritionist" who also held a diploma mill degree. The National News Council which investigates deceptive and misleading information in the print media, looked into the matter after receiving complaints. They found the complaints to be justified. They also learned that the author already had two criminal convictions relating to nutrition fraud. He had received a sentence of two years summary probation for each of them. At the time, the very questionable institution from which this man had received his degree operated in apparent full compliance with state statutes in California (Herbert, 1982, p. 245).

In a 1983 article in the journal *Health Values*, nutritionists Victor Herbert, William T. Jarvis, and Grace Powers Monaco defined the problem of diploma mill fraud in their profession. They identified five states—California, Nevada, Oregon, Florida, and Illinois—as particular sources of diploma mill-related nutrition fraud. Suspect educational practices were producing unqualified nutritionists, nutrition counselors, nutrition consultants, natural health-care practitioners, and holistic practitioners. Typically the pitch to prospective students was sales oriented, designed to prepare someone to sell food supplements, herbs, or other "health foods." Authors of textbooks and institutional "faculty" were generally in the business of producing or selling "health foods." Such terms as "natural," "holistic," "nutrition doctor," and "health food" were frequently used—no sin in itself except that their meanings had been distorted because of widespread abuse of the terms in the distribution of questionable products and in practice.

Legitimate nutritionists and the public do not always have potent legal weapons to combat this type of predatory behavior. In California, for example, the state's Business and Professions Code (Section 2068) specifies that anyone may give nutritional advice as long as its does not constitute diagnosis or treatment. Any "consultant" may give advice or counsel. Only diagnosis and treatment are prohibited—activities that such consultants can scrupulously avoid.

The personalized nutrition racket is another variation on the diploma mill theme. Scientific nutrition, just for you, is the enticement here. Customers in a health food or vitamin store are asked to fill out a questionnaire. Results are then fed into a computer, which turns out the names of foods carried in the store that are alleged to be required by the customer. On prominent display in many such stores are Ph.D. diplomas awarded by a nutrition credential diploma mill. Phony credentials are used to coax money from the unsuspecting and to help persuade members of the public to buy products that are unnecessary or possibly even harmful (Herbert, Jarvis, and Monaco, 1985, p. 246).

In the words of Victor Herbert, who has investigated nutrition fraud, most such products are "nothing more than snake oil remedies, which bilk a gullible public of billions annually." Law enforcement officials, however, are hesitant about prosecuting under laws that often require unanimous decisions by a jury and jail for the offenders. The majority of cases relating to nutrition fraud are therefore tried under charges that can result in a lesser penalty (Herbert, Jarvis, and Monaco, 1985, p. 247).

Certainly one of the most charming "Nutritional Consultants" in the United States is Rebecca Jean Lawhead who acquired her papers from "The American Association of Nutritional Consultants" at the age of 5. At age 6 (see photo), she is still a "professional member" in good standing. Rebecca's mother, Clara Lawhead, Nutrition Director of the Pasco County (Florida) Health Department (and also a certified public health nutritionist and registered dietician), submitted an application for Rebecca to demonstrate how easy it is to obtain a designation as "nutritionist" without having appropriate experience or credentials. Similar success in achieving nutrition consultant status has been achieved by at least two dogs and one cat (Meyers, 1984, p. 116; Staats, 1983).

The National Council Against Health Fraud (see Appendix B) is actively working to combat the problem of nutrition education fraud. It focuses on "health fraud, misinformation and quackery as consumer health problems." Council members, who include registered dietitians (17.5 percent of the total membership) and medical doctors (12 percent) serve as expert witnesses in court and serve as members of a speaker's bureau and do research to provide information for consumer protection articles.

Education. The profession of education has not been growing in recent years and a number of schools of education have attenuated their programs. However, the field qualifies as a hot spot for diploma mill operators because of the sheer

Rebecca Jean Lawhead of Odessa, Florida, qualified as a "nutritional consultant" at age 5. At age 6 when this photo was taken, she was still a "Professional Member" in good standing of "The American Association of Nutritional Consultants."

numbers of practicing educators. Education systems and institutions (including primary and secondary schools) place a high premium on advanced degrees. Often, a diploma mill master's degree or Ph.D. can be a guaranteed ticket to a higher position or salary.

On the other hand, a diploma mill degree can also lead

to disgrace and imprisonment. When the FBI closed down diploma mills operated by Anthony Geruntino and others, it discovered the names of about 2000 persons who had bought the phony degrees. Many of the undergraduate and graduate degrees were in education.

Religion. Religion has always provided built-in attractions for diploma mills though such endeavors are not always invidious in intent. To congregations unsophisticated in the protocols of academic nomenclature, the title "Doctor" for their pastor sounds very good indeed, and they may encourage him or her to acquire the title from an educational organization that they perceive reflects their own religious doctrines.

Sometimes, too, a church may set up an institute or college which performs a legitimate function in training its missionaries or church workers. Later, the enterprise may branch out to award degrees other than an authorized one in religion. Either way, state statutes may be violated unintentionally by bonafide religious organizations, as well as intentionally by those who use religion as a cover for fraudulent higher education.

Religious programs and institutions are often exempt from regulation under state statutes. Diploma mill sharks can sometimes use a religious institutional designation (e.g., "Christian") to award degrees in a wide variety of subjects in the liberal arts, sciences, or professional fields, along with degrees bearing religious designations. In Virginia, for example, the relatively tough laws, assertively enforced, that govern authorization of degree-granting institutions can sometimes be circumvented by the clever use of religious labels for an institution and its program on the papers submitted for state authorization.

Many instant doctors of theology join the faculty or administration of their "alma mater" and begin selling degrees and reaping profits in earnest. The art involves more than just awarding degrees. A religious-sounding name can also provide a good mask for phony sexual therapy, marriage counseling, sale of religious articles, and other activities that are not encouraged in the Bible.

Consequences

What are the principal consequences of the present frenetic pace of diploma mill activity? There are at least three: devaluation of legitimate American academic degrees, damaging consumer fraud, and employer fraud.

American institutions of higher education suffer as a result of the widespread activity by diploma mills. The integrity of genuine degrees—all of them—is threatened. Pressures build on legitimate institutions to water down their programs to compete with institutions that do not have high standards.

Every time a diploma mill awards a degree for little or no academic achievement, the environment surrounding the people who hold legitimate degrees of that kind is poisoned. In the eyes of some, the American baccalaureate degree is already virtually meaningless, in part because of its perversion by diploma mill operators. Public confidence in American institutions of higher education has begun to erode. In foreign countries, too, the credibility of American higher education has received a black eye.

In addition to cheapened degrees, consumer fraud is a severe problem. Members of the public are cheated whenever they are treated by or otherwise served by persons who do not have the knowledge or skills their credentials suggest. Consider the holders of fraudulent degrees who were conducting cancer seminars, or the one conducting cervical and breast examinations and telling patients they had a precancerous condition. One woman was charged $30,000 for the privilege of going to Mexico and using laetrile. These examples were uncovered by FBI agents in 1985 (McQuaid, April 1985, pp. 52–53).

Fraudulent degrees can threaten public safety on a broader scale as well. For example, degrees in environmental safety and health, fire science, and occupational health and safety are offered by more than one highly questionable institution.

Employers, and sometimes the public, suffer when employees who are unprepared to do their appointed jobs are hired. Employers also suffer when their present employees are granted promotions or higher salaries resulting from diploma mill credentials. In view of this drain on employers it is surprising that so few of them bother to screen applicants' credentials except when filling highly professional or technical positions.

As shown, the problem of diploma mill activity in the United States is a complicated one. Given the prevailing societal trends and pressures, it is likely to get worse in the absence of corrective action. But the cures that some prescribe could be worse than the disease itself.

The key question facing the nation now is this: How can the integrity of academic degrees in America be maintained without discouraging innovation aimed at meeting the needs of new groups of clients? How, too, can the brakes be put on diploma mills without developing rigid proscriptive mechanisms either inside the academic establishment or within government agencies that have regulatory jurisdiction over certain aspects of postsecondary education?

In order to develop answers, we must first recognize and engage the perpetrators of the problem.

3

Characteristics of a Diploma Mill: How to Know One When You See One

Achieving the appearance of legitimacy is among the first tasks that serious diploma mill operators must master. Getting state authorization under less than stringent laws is a great help if the organization expects to function legally. Operators will usually seek authorization from a state where the laws relating to authorization are weak or virtually nonexistent. They will then attempt to make state authorization and/or higher state approval sound as if it is equivalent to accreditation. Sometimes COPA-recognized accreditation is portrayed as a mere "alternative" that is not chosen by the institution.

In the absence of accreditation or candidacy from a COPA-recognized agency, other avenues of achieving the appearance of accreditation review must be explored. One route is "accreditation" by an entity that is nothing more than an accreditation mill. But there are other ways for the cleverest of diploma mill operators.

Setting up a dummy governing board is one innovative approach. One of the legally operating California institutions established a board of regents that seems less than active. One member, a state government official, was never notified of her appointment. She resigned from the board after learning by chance that her name was one of those billed as providing "advice and counsel" to the administration.

In the same category is the phony advisory committee. Some very prominent members of the American Speech–Language–Hearing Association (ASHA) were recently astonished and dismayed to learn they had been named as "Advisory Board Members" for a newly formed nontraditional doctoral program at an authorized, but unaccredited, California institution. In an open letter appearing in ASHA's journal, these four individuals stated that their names were being used without permission. When invited, they said they had agreed to serve as consultants "to assist in the *planning*" of a program proposal. Instead, they were presented with a *fait accompli*. A program was launched and their names were being used without authorization. In a body, the group resigned as consultants (*Asha*, 1985, p. 5).

ACE, the major umbrella education association to which most American colleges and universities belong, found itself infiltrated under its little noticed "affiliate member" category. Screening procedures for this category of membership were subsequently tightened after it was discovered that several highly questionable organizations (including Anthony Geruntino's homemade university) had become affiliates. These organizations went on to imply in their catalogs and promotional material that their organizations had ACE endorsement.

Publishing long lists of industries, institutions, and agencies whose current or previous employees have been enrolled in a diploma mill is another effective technique for achieving the appearance of legitimacy. Sometimes these lists are accompanied by excerpts from letters of officials who appear to have acknowledged routine inquiries about whether or not they would employ graduates of a questionable organization. Careful reading of these statements suggests that they are nothing more than a willingness to "consider" hiring or promoting such individuals.

Advertising is the lifeblood of the diploma mill business. Their ads shout their messages from hundreds of publications of all types. They may appear in the most respectable publications, often alongside advertisements for legitimate institutions. Airline magazines appear to be a particular favorite. Mentioned as carrying diploma mill advertisements in some of the FBI's 1987 Dipscam indictments are these publications: *National Enquirer, Star, National Examiner, Globe, Popular Mechanics, Psychology Today,* and *Psychology Magazine* (U.S. vs. Fowler, 3 December 1986; U.S. vs. Pany, 3 February 1986).

These days, the usual target is adults who feel stymied, either professionally or personally, by an absence of credentials. The award of credit for "life experience" is often the prime come-on. Applicants are encouraged to think that such an evaluation will result in an award of nearly all credits necessary for the degree being sought, and this premise is often accurate. The prestige of college or advanced degrees may also be highlighted.

Hard-hitting and shrewdly targeted advertising is essential for the success of a diploma mill. Diploma mill tycoon Anthony Geruntino perhaps put it best in his testimony before a Congressional subcommittee: "the lifeline to any bogus school or institution that operates primarily by mail, and its lifeblood is the advertising and their mailing lists. Without those two items there basically is no market. . . Without a mailing list, without the ability to advertise, a [diploma mill] will dry up." (U.S. Congress, House, 11 December 1985, p. 54).

Typical of advertising placed by Geruntino was an ad in

Popular Mechanics which offered "UNIVERSITY DE-
GREES BY SPECIAL EVALUATION OF EXISTING Job
Experience, Education, Achievement. Fast, Inexpensive,"
(U.S. Congress, House, 11 December 1985, p. 195).

Ads or promotional materials may also highlight prestige, for example, suggesting that friends will be impressed
by anyone who is even enrolled in a professional or career
college-level program. The ease with which such degrees can
be obtained is emphasized, with particular reference to the
absence of the need to attend classes.

In testimony at a 1984 hearing sponsored by the Subcommittee on Health and Long-term Care of the House Select
Committee on Aging, it was revealed that Pedro de Mesones,
a convicted diploma mill operator, had placed ads in *The New
York Times* and the *Los Angeles Times*, among other publications. These messages were targeted at would-be medical
students who had failed to gain entrance to American medical
schools. The proposed solution to their dilemmas: letters of
good standing, recommendations, transcripts and degrees from
off-shore medical schools in Caribbean countries—all without
attendance, (U.S. Congress, House, 7 December 1984, pp.
133–145).

Diploma mills are notorious for emulating in a most su-
perficial way the structures and functions of legitimate programs under which people earn degrees. Conversely, many
legitimate colleges and universities are now offering programs
that are nontraditional when set against more conventional
courses of study in higher education. An institution accredited
by an agency recognized by the Council on Postsecondary
Accreditation (COPA) may have no campus, for example. Or
this institution may use part-time faculty as it adapts its programs to meet the needs of adult learners.

By understanding the reasons behind these strategies,
it is possible to develop a list of characteristics of a diploma
mill operation. If presented with prudence and caution, the
following characteristics may sometimes (not always!) be cited
as typical of diploma mills in the United States. Few of them
alone, however, are enough to relegate a particular organization to diploma mill status.

Name/Address/Mail

1. The organization may have a name similar to that of a well-known college or university. (The following examples of this practice by "mail order degree granting schools" are cited in the official record of a hearing held by the U.S. House of Representatives Select Committee on Aging, Subcommittees on Health and Long-Term Care and Housing and Consumer Interests, in December of 1985: "Stamford University, not Stanford University; Cormell University, not Cornell University; Darthmouth, instead of Dartmouth; Boston City College, instead of Boston College; Northwestern College of Allied Science of Tulsa, Oklahoma, instead of Northwestern College of Evanstown [sic], Illinois; Cambridge University of Washington, D.C., instead of Cambridge University of Cambridge, England; Southwestern University of Tucson, Arizona and Columbus, Ohio, instead of Southwestern University of Georgetown, Texas; Thomas A. Edison College of Florida and Arkansas, instead of Thomas A. Edison College of Trenton, New Jersey; American National University of Phoenix, Arizona, and American National University of Miami, Florida, instead of American University of Washington, D.C.; Southeastern University of Greenville, North Carolina, instead of Southeastern University of Washington, D.C." [U.S. Congress, House, 11 December 1985, p. 138].)

2. The address often suggests a prestigious location. However, mail may be received only at a postal box number.

3. Mail may be received at the address of a mail-forwarding service.

4. The organization may frequently change its address, sometimes moving from state to state.

5. The organization's use of adjectives can be tricky. For example, the terms "United States" or "U.S." used in the names of a college or university can be misinterpreted, particularly by foreigners, to convey official government sanction.

6. The word "international" often appears in the organization's name or program description as a means of denoting prestige or as a justification for far-flung program activity.

Anthony Geruntino's "Southwestern University" retreated from its campus at Tucson (top) when Arizona tightened its statutes governing the operation of colleges and universities but set up shop again in St. George in Utah (bottom) where laws are more permissive. (Courtesy of Federal Bureau of Investigation.)

Catalog/Promotional Literature

1. Catalogs of questionable organizations can give subtly false impressions of the goods purveyed within. One organization, for example, carries on its cover handsome photographs of the civic center and other showcase buildings in the community in which it is located. In the absence of identification, prospective students are led to believe that this is a photograph taken on the campus of the institution. The actual locale of this organization at the time the catalog was published was a modest second floor office in a building where other tenants included a credit collection agency and an acupuncture clinic.

2. Narrative in catalogs and promotional materials may be filled with errors in spelling, grammar, and syntax. (A particular favorite of the authors of this volume is a Ph.D. in "Scared Theology" that is promised in the catalog of one organization.)

3. The catalog is filled with extravagant or pretentious language, for example, the generous and often inappropriate or awkward use of such words as "didactis" or "symposia."

4. Catalogs are long on Latin, which is frequently on letterheads as well.

5. It is stated in the catalog that each student's dissertation is placed on file in the Library of Congress. (The Library of Congress uses commercial subscription services to acquire information about dissertations and lengthy research papers. Such acquisition, of course, implies no certification of quality.)

6. A photograph of the diploma appears in the organization's catalog or promotional literature.

7. A sample copy of a diploma is used in promotional mailings to prospective students.

8. The catalog contains numerous photographs showing the award of honorary degrees to prominent local figures.

Policies/Procedures/Requirements

1. There is little or no selectivity in admissions; frequently, no admissions requirements are listed, and there is

no evidence that the organization has the services available to support operation under a sound open-admissions policy. If an open-admissions policy exists, there is no evidence that sound or rigorous criteria for graduation have been established.

2. Catalog descriptions of programs grossly vary from the reality of the programs actually offered.

3. A wide range of degrees with a dazzling array of impressive titles is offered. Frequently a special degree title not listed in the catalog can be obtained without evidence that the institution has resources that could support this type of individualized major.

4. Degree requirements, if any, are few and are frequently unspecified.

5. Assessment of learning outcomes or achievement is minimal or nonexistent.

6. Professional advanced degrees may be acquired without clearly established examination for requirements and assessment designed to assure mastery of knowledge and skills in the field.

7. Degrees ordinarily can be obtained in a time frame far shorter than that required for completion of a program at a generally recognized and COPA-agency accredited institution. Often degrees are awarded within a few weeks or months from the time of enrollment, without evidence that the organization has in place a sound program of assessing prior learning, support for self-directed study, and so on.

8. Degrees may be backdated.

9. Dissertations, rather than being structured analyses based on original research, may take the form of a shallow analysis or descriptions of various aspects of a person's job or current life situation. Dissertations are accepted with misspelled words and grammatical errors.

10. Dissertations or other scholarly works are not defended before acknowledged scholars in the field.

11. Quantity, rather than quality, apparently prevails at one questionable institution which cites one student as pos-

sessing the distinction of writing the "largest" dissertation on record at the institution. A California institution awarded a doctorate to a student who spent two months logging, without analysis, broadcasts of the television program "Sesame Street."

12. Student work is not done under appropriate academic or professional supervision.

13. In the case of diploma reproduction services, the duplicate or simulated diploma for a legitimate college or university may carry a written disclaimer so placed that it can be completely covered by a frame.

Faculty/Administration/Staff

1. Governing boards may not exist or may be composed of persons unqualified to serve in such positions. Some persons listed as board members may not know of their appointments to the board. (One diploma mill operator acquired a do-it-yourself Ph.D. from his own board of directors: his mother and an unemployed janitor.)

2. There is often a preoccupation with degree-identification for individuals listed in the catalog or promotional literature. Long lists of degrees typically follow the names of all officials (for example: John Doe, Chancellor, Ph.D., Ed.D., B.S.Ed., M.A.R., D.D., L.H.D., L.L.D.) A recent review of ACE files on diploma mill organizations revealed one individual listing a record number of nine Ph.D. degrees after his name.

3. Few programs have full-time staff with the appropriate academic qualifications to serve as professional educators or administrators in academic programs.

4. Many or all faculty lack appropriate advanced degrees from generally recognized and COPA-agency accredited higher education institutions. A number of faculty members may hold advanced degrees from the diploma mill itself or from similar organizations.

5. Some individuals listed as faculty members may not teach any course, nor provide any services for the institution. In some instances, these individuals may not even know they are listed as faculty by the organization. (Their names may have been obtained through advertisements for adjunct or part-time appointments directed to retired faculty from legitimate colleges and universities. The impressive qualifications of these individuals may be listed in promotional literature without the knowledge or consent that their names are being used.)

6. Part-time staff, most of whom are full-time employees of other organizations, are used heavily to provide instruction or academic services. There is no evidence that such part-time staff have strong ties to the organization or that they function under appropriate orientation, supervision, and evaluation procedures. Also such staff members may not meet the same or comparable requirements for professional, experiential, and scholarly preparation as their full-time counterparts (if any) teaching in the same disciplines.

Nontraditional Program Abuses

1. Great emphasis is placed upon granting credit for work experience and prior life experience without appropriate mechanisms for assessing that experience in terms of college-level learning. Also, little emphasis is given to relating such experience and learning to specified degree requirements. Sometimes the assessment is offered free to prospective students on a casual mail-order basis with an implicit promise that much more credit than is anticipated may be awarded upon actual enrollment. (See chapter 5 for a detailed explanation of this type of abuse.)

2. Terms such as "nontraditional," "alternative," and "innovative" are generously used to gloss over a multitude of academic sins. Respected programs such as those offered by the Council for the Advancement of Adult and Experiential Learning (CAEL), the College-Level Examination Program (CLEP) of the College Board, and the American Council on Education (ACE) may be used without any explanations of the principles involved.

3. Sometimes the appearance of quality is enough to mislead. For example, the ACE publishes guidelines for use by institutions engaging in the assessment and award of credit for prior experiential learning. An institution attempting to defraud the public could mention that it has "adopted" these guidelines, may even publish them in full in its promotional materials, while ignoring them in practice.

4. Many of the organization's degrees are awarded to students in remote, often exotic, locations, such as Saudi Arabia, Ethiopia, or India.

Authorization/Approval/Accreditation

1. The organization is not accredited by an agency recognized by the Council on Postsecondary Accreditation (COPA) or the U.S. Department of Education. Promotional materials may, however, report accreditation by organizations that do not have such recognition and that under present circumstances are unlikely ever to have it.

2. The words "licensed," "state-authorized," or "state-approved" are used to suggest (erroneously) that the organization has undergone a process of academic review comparable to accreditation.

3. The organization may be authorized under laws of one state but have its principal base of operations in another state.

Fiscal

1. Tuition and fees are typically on a per degree basis rather than a per semester, per quarter, or per course basis. For example, a bachelor's degree might cost $1,000; a master's degree, $1,800; and a doctoral degree, $2,200. Frequently, this information is stated on application forms and most or all the payment is expected to be sent in advance.

2. Prospective students may be sent letters urging them to "enroll now" before an increase in fee or tuition takes effect. These letters may be routinely sent to anyone whose reply to an earlier letter is not received within a given period of time.

3. Prospective students who do not respond to an early

recruiting letter are sent another letter notifying them that they have qualified for a "fellowship," "scholarship," or "grant" that will mean a lowered fee or tuition upon enrollment. One person, a resident of the African nation of Zambia, reports that he received such a "scholarship" because he lived in a third-world country.

4. In the catalog a refund of fee or tuition is offered to anyone not satisfied with the degree issued.

Facilities

1. The organization frequently operates from a single room in a private home or in an office building and has no formal arrangements for the use of facilities and services that it does not own.

2. The organization does not maintain a library of sufficient breadth and depth to support its programs; nor is there provision for access to non-owned libraries. No guidance for using libraries or other resources is provided to the student.

With these broad brush strokes, a portrait of the institutions of academic fraud begins to emerge.

4

By the Numbers:
An Art, Not a Science

How many diploma mills are currently active in the United States? This is the first question usually asked by almost any type of audience in a presentation about diploma mills. The honest answer is that no one really knows, and it is unlikely that an empirically sound answer will ever be obtained.

Furthermore, the question itself implies the existence of an answer that would be misleading even if the numbers could be obtained. It cannot be said that a moribund mill has been rendered harmless. Such organizations by definition tend to resurface in one form or another, so it is unwise to describe them at any time as permanently out of business.

Like bad pennies, diploma mills return to cause trouble. Even if the organization is no longer issuing diplomas, the fraudulent products of the past are still being used. For example, the Ohio Board of Regents which oversees all of post-secondary education in the state, still receives inquiries about

"Ohio Christian College," a notorious diploma mill that was never authorized to operate in Ohio and that was put out of business by the Federal Trade Commission (FTC) in 1971. So many inquiries are received that even sixteen years afterward, the Board uses a form letter to respond (Skinner, 1987). The long-closed Ohio Christian College is, it seems, still active because its "alumni" still cite the diplomas it awarded years ago.

The imprecise definition of the term "diploma mill" presents a further barrier to rational development of statistics. Does one include only illegal organizations? If certain legal organizations are included, what criteria govern their inclusion? Are foreign diploma mills operating in this country to be included? This list of shoulds and shouldn'ts goes on.

Diploma mills themselves tend to resist statistical definition. Neither they, nor their clients, are necessarily anxious to broadcast news that may cause them trouble. For all of these reasons, the presentation of statistics about the diploma mill problem must be considered an art and not a science. Informed estimates must be the norm defining the problem. Over the years, there have been many of these informed estimates.

Benjamin Fine in a *New York Times* article in 1950 said there were more than 1,000 diploma mills, over 100 of which were degree-granting (Reid, 1964, p. 110). In 1959, in his study commissioned by ACE, Robert Reid pinpointed about 200 diploma mills in thirty-seven states and suggested that nearly one million persons had been enrolled in these organizations (Reid, 1964, pp. 40–41).

The U.S. Office of Education in 1960 issued a list of degree mills that included some twenty-five organizations in nine states. Another ten organizations were cited as "chartered in the United States" but active abroad (Reid, 1964, pp. 11–12).

By 1972, John R. Proffitt, Director of Accreditation and Institutional Eligibility of the U.S. Office of Education, had found 110 schools that he would identify as diploma mills. In his 1972 book *Degrees for Sale*, Lee Porter said that the number of diploma mills then in existence might easily exceed 200 (Porter, 1972, p. 6).

In testimony before a Congressional subcommittee in December 1985, Anthony Geruntino, a diploma mill operator himself, made a conservative estimate that there were about 150 diploma mills in America, each of which was awarding about 3,000 diplomas before being caught. Geruntino himself awarded some 2,000 diplomas over a five-year period and grossed approximately 2 million dollars (U.S. Congress, House, 11 December 1985, pp. 51–52).

The FBI in 1984 estimated that there were at least 100 organizations that it would define as illegal diploma mills in the United States, selling a total of 10,000 to 15,000 degrees per year (McGrath, 1984, p. 90). Some hints as to the volume of this traffic in the recent past appear in the FBI's record of its action against an organization called Alumni Arts in Grants Pass, Oregon. According to FBI Special Agent Otho Allen Ezell, Jr., more than 2,300 persons purchased diplomas bearing the names of about 200 legitimate educational institutions from this organization. Alumni Arts apparently expected, or was experiencing, a boom in business. The customers of Alumni Arts were, for the most part, fully aware of the fraudulent nature of the sales transaction. About 30,000 blank pieces of diploma paper were acquired when the FBI confiscated the organization's business records (Ezell interview, 1985).

E. Patrick McQuaid, a former journalist now a staff member at the Education Commission of the States, reports that he acquired seven diplomas from Alumni Arts while doing research for an article on diploma mills that appeared in *Science* in 1985. The institutions whose diplomas were counterfeited, according to McQuaid, were Harvard University, Babson College, American University of Beirut, Central New England College of Technology, University of Massachusetts at Boston, American College in Jerusalem, and Universidad de la Habana (McQuaid interview, 1987).

In 1981, Dr. Lyn Gubser, then Director of the National Council for Accreditation of Teacher Education (NCATE), said that some 18 percent of all education doctorates awarded

in 1979–1980 were of the "quickie degree" variety conferred
by institutions lacking COPA-recognized accreditation. The
total number of such suspect doctorates in education was 1,350.
NCATE's survey of questionable institutions for the same
year (1979–1980) revealed that most organizations were gross-
ing between $100,000 and $300,000 a year. The smallest institution among those surveyed took in $65,700 (Gubser, 1982,
pp. 15–25).

What is the situation today vis-a-vis diploma mills? What
can be safely said about their numbers? And, finally, what is
the number of diploma mills in relation to the number of legitimate colleges and universities?

According to the 1986–1987 edition of *Accredited Institutions of Postsecondary Education*, some 5,156 American
postsecondary education institutions have accreditation by an
agency recognized by COPA. Of these, 2,006 are four-year
colleges or universities, 1,360 are two-year colleges, 1,613 are
nondegree-granting institutions, and 177 hold "candidacy for
accreditation" status (Harris, 1986–1987).

It is not easy to enter and define the realm of diploma
mills and related organizations. ACE has, however, collected information on some 357 organizations that it considers at least questionable based on criteria stated in chapter
3. For example, all of these organizations grant degrees in
a much shorter time frame than ordinarily considered adequate for appropriate academic accomplishment by generally recognized postsecondary education institutions. Many
mills operate from a post office box or mail-forwarding service. Many move a number of times. All appear to have far
fewer resources than would seem necessary to deliver quality degree programs of the types listed. It must be emphasized, however, that this aggregation of data is not a complete inventory or even a scientific sample and is not being
presented as such.

This information has been collected over a period of six
years via:

1. Review of catalogs or related materials obtained directly
   from the organizations or other sources

2. Personal observation by ACE staff members or staff members of other higher education associations and institutions
3. FBI, U.S. Postal Inspection Service, Congressional or other federal government documents
4. State governmental or educational agencies
5. Personnel officials of businesses or other employers
6. Reports or questions submitted by aggrieved consumers
7. Directory listings
8. Newspaper clippings.

Some of these sources cannot be considered completely reliable in any empirical or scholarly sense.

Some forty-three organizations in the group apparently operate (or did operate) legally under the laws of their state of domicile. Another 126 organizations operate (or did operate) illegally. The status of the remaining organizations is unknown, but is probably illegal in most instances.

Many of these organizations offer bachelor's, master's, and doctoral degrees in a wide variety of subjects. Some confine themselves to offering degrees in a particular field, such as doctorates in psychology or education. Combined degrees are frequently available, including B.A./M.A. or M.A./Ph.D. programs. (One organization even offers a complete B.A./M.A./Ph.D. program.) A relatively small number (42) offer the associate of arts (A.A.) degree as well, and fewer still (34) offer high school diplomas. With the exception of those few organizations that seem to offer them as a specialty, the usual diploma mill shies away from offering degrees in medicine or law.

Some of the organizations in the ACE sample offer degree "add-ons," such as transcripts, letters of recommendation, and diploma "replacement." The transcript "service" appears to be associated primarily with the bargain-basement diploma mill. A number of organizations that offer degrees or diplomas for less than $200, also offer transcripts.

The typical organization offers few or no classes on its premises. Off campus classes or activities of some kind are another matter. At least seventy-seven have what appear to be substantial activities off campus. At least seventy of these include activity in states other than the one of domicile and at least twenty-six appear to have substantial operations overseas.

If the organizations in the ACE sample are sorted by state, they tend to cluster in just eleven states. However, this clustering is misleading as an index of activity without some qualification. For example, the sample extends over a six-year period and includes states such as Arizona where a new law is now in effect. Arizona's twenty-six diploma mills all predated the new law and, so far as is known, are not now in operation.

With its total ninety-three, California tops the list of states having apparent diploma mills for reasons explained in detail in chapter 11. Essentially, this number stems from a now-amended law that made it all too easy to incorporate and be authorized or approved to operate as a college or a university. The new law is tougher and the state's Private Postsecondary Education Division is trying to clean house—to the extent this is possible since some questionable organizations are firmly entrenched. The ACE sample does *not* include all or even most institutions now authorized or approved to operate in California but not holding COPA-recognized accreditation. It *does* include some institutions possessing many of the characteristics stated as typical of diploma mills, as well as organizations now closed but having "alumni" who can cite their degrees.

Florida, with forty-three apparent diploma mills, also has disproportionately high representation in the sample. Extremely weak laws governing authorization of educational institutions have been tightened to some degree. However, the state's past history of permissiveness cannot be erased.

Missouri with nineteen institutions in the sample is in fourth place. Some of these organizations are still operational and completely legal under some of the nation's weakest regulatory statutes.

The shadowy nature of many organizations makes precise information about their fees elusive. The catalogs often are not revised yearly and are intended to last for several years.

Information about their fees is therefore presented in the same fashion. Nonetheless, we can generalize with confidence about the usual fee structures. The fees charged are usually expressed as a flat amount *per degree*, although occasionally, the charge is expressed per year or per credit unit.

A bi-modal distribution characterizes the fee structure for those organizations that charge a flat fee for a bachelor of arts degree. Since 1984, most such fees fall into two groups: those charging between $1,200 and $1,999 for a B.A. and those charging between $2,000 and $3,000. At the high end of the scale, one organization charged $5,390 for a B.S. The rock-bottom price was $175 which would go to a printer of diplomas, not to a more sophisticated diploma mill.

Between 1982 and 1983, one could obtain B.A.'s for $10, $39.95, $40, or $85, if all one wanted was a piece of parchment. Stepping up to an ersatz university meant entering a price range of $1,000 to $2,500, with an average of $1,695. Backing up to 1980–1981 the price range for a baccalaureate degree posing as higher education becomes $1,000 to $1,600.

The same institutions that were practically giving away B.A. degrees at $40 were also printing M.A.'s as fast as they could, perhaps for $5.00 more (or $45). Other institutions tacked on $100 or $200, going from $1,695 for a B.A. to $1,795 or $1,895 for M.A.'s. A few institutions charged top dollar for a master's degree, asking $3,500 or $3,750.

Since 1984, however, flat fees for a master's degree have mostly been in the $1,250–$3,700 range. One institution aggressively marketed its M.A. at $8,300–$9,300; another parted with its degree for only $200.

Going back a bit farther, master's degrees were a bargain in 1980 and 1981. Almost no one was charging over $2,000; most charged between $100 and $350.

Doctoral degrees, especially the Ph.D. and M.D., are the high-ticket items in the diploma mill inventory. By 1984, a store-bought M.D. was costing $35,000 from one operator while up to $27,000 was asked by another. A careful shopper, however, could save a good deal of money on a Ph.D. Although it was easy to drop $4,000–$5,000, just as many discount operations offered a Ph.D. from $2,000–$3,000, while a third

group, about the same size, found its niche at the $3,000–
$4,000 range. A doctor of jurisprudence (J.D.) might cost
$4,800. At bargain basement prices ($100, $150, or $250) a
phony Ph.D. could be yours from a few hustlers.

Between 1982–1983 a Ph.D. was either very expensive
or very cheap. At the high end were two ranges with consumers tending to pay $10,000–$13,750, and about $5,000–
$6,000 for their diplomas. Mid-range prices in the entire sam-
ple were about $1,200–$1,995. A bigger market evidently existed for Ph.D. diplomas that cost $39.95 or $40—or, if not a
bigger market, at least more of the parties responsible for
those bargain scams have been caught.

For under $1,000, a phony Ph.D. was readily available
between 1980–1981. Of course, one could always spend the
$45,600 charged for an M.D./D.V.M. (Doctor of Veterinary
Medicine) by one outfit. Or, if medicine seemed exorbitant,
an L.L.B. degree (Bachelor of Laws) was on the market for
just $200.

Not many of these organizations specialize in offering
associate degrees. Those that do charge a flat fee between
$150 and $2,500; or they charge a per semester hour fee of
$50 to $100. Before 1984, flat fees ranged from $90 to $500.

Not many operators specialized in high school diplomas.
The going rate has ranged from $75 to $650. For "only" $15,
one outfit provided high school equivalency examination practice tests, material that at the time was available more cheaply
(and legally) from the GED Testing Service.

Some organizations charge a flat fee per year for degrees.
For instance, a B.A. could cost anywhere from $1,800 to $4,200
per year. The majority that charge per year do so on a per
credit hour or per course unit basis. This fee has remained
steady over the years at about $50 per unit for a B.A. The
fee per year for a master's degree has ranged from $1,600 to
$5,000. The per credit hour price is greater for an M.A. than
a B.A., ranging from $50 to $165.

The fee per year for a doctorate has ranged from $1,800
to $5,000, with the average fee somewhat steeper than for an
M.A. The per course units have been approximately the same
as for M.A. degrees.

Combined degree programs are a specialty at some diploma mills. In recent years, the going rate for a B.A./M.A. combined degree has been about $3,800. Early in the 1980s, the fee went as low as $2,095 and as high as $6,000.

An M.A./Ph.D. has been running between $3,000 and $4,760. In the early 1980s, the price ranged from $2,175 to $9,000.

Other unusual educational offers made by various institutions were a Ph.D./J.D. for $2,875; a B.A./Ph.D. for $2,595; a B.A./M.A./Ph.D. for $3,565; and a B.S./M.S./Ph.D. for $5,495.

Some institutions offer financing for students at commercial interest rates which, of course, would boost profits considerably, and some organizations say that financial aid is available. Some have higher interest rates for foreign students. Discounts for two or more degrees are not unusual. Many offer related "services" that add to the total cost of a degree.

As can be seen, it pays to shop around for a diploma mill degree—but the lowest price is not the only consideration. One should also consider the value of appearance, since some diploma mill parchment can look very much like the real thing.

5
The Threat to Nontraditional Higher Education

The pluralistic state of American postsecondary education is at once a strength and a weakness. With its inherent flexibility and pragmatic orientation, the system puts a premium on healthy innovation and imagination. But this very pragmatism and flexibility can cause confusion as well, for they make it possible for diploma mills to flourish under the banner of innovation and outreach.

In recent years, many diploma mills have advertised themselves as "nontraditional" and in the forefront of efforts to make higher education more useful and more accessible to people having adult responsibilities. Deception and fraud is often implicit in such an approach and may not be fully understood by those

45

unfamiliar with new developments in higher education. Herein lies the threat to legitimate nontraditional education.

The term "nontraditional study," as generally used in postsecondary education circles, incorporates credit programs based on new or unconventional forms of education that are free of time, place, and space limitations typical of traditional classroom-based instruction. In specific terms, such legitimate programs may be unconventional in any of the following ways:

- The students enrolled may be working adults, house-wives, young or older adults motivated to study independently, or others who cannot easily come to the campus or who cannot or do not wish to devote full time to class-room endeavors.
- The location of the learning experience may be unusual in that it takes place off campus in a regional learning center, field work location, an office or factory, or even in the learner's home.
- Policies and procedures may provide maximum recognition of prior, college-level learning, regardless of the manner by which such learning was attained.
- The method of instruction may involve media, (e.g., computers, satellites, audiographics, video cassettes), programmed learning materials, or other nonclassroom methods that have not been commonly practiced within postsecondary education institutions.
- The content of the program may be either the same or different from conventional campus courses or programs, but in either instance, it must be a program offered for atypical students or at an unusual location or presented in a novel way.
- The institutional arrangements for student support services such as counseling or for instruction may incorporate contractual relationships with organizations (e.g., business and industry, labor unions, professional associations) or individuals not previously having direct ties to the institution.
- Other characteristics often found in nontraditional programs include competency-based curricula, reduced or no-

residency requirements for earning a degree, and greater participation by students in designing their own learning programs and experiences.

A number of relatively unfamiliar terms have been introduced to describe some of these instruments of nontraditional learning. Among these are: (1) assessment of experiential learning, (2) external degree, (3) evaluations of formal training, (4) portfolio development, (5) contract learning, (6) competency-based curriculum, and (7) correspondence study. Brief explanations of these terms and some examples of their distortion by diploma mills follow. (Full references for the key resources discussed in this chapter are included in Appendix C.)

Assessment of Experiential Learning

Perhaps the most egregious sin committed by diploma mills is that of assigning credit for experiential learning without using proper procedures for assuring documentation and methods of assessing whether or not such learning actually occurred and represents college-level performance. Credits approved for transfer into an institution's program may be based on simple "clock hours" or statements of time spent in a particular job or learning situation. For example, service of one, two, or three years in a particular job may be assigned proportionally increasing increments of credit—without any effort to assess the real nature of the job, the skills and knowledge it requires, its qualifications, or theoretical understanding in it.

When it is done with integrity, prior learning assessment is not a casual process. Information is collected and presented in a systematic way. Appropriate documentation procedures are spelled out and followed; assessment techniques appropriate to the learning are applied by faculty. Credit is not assigned on a wholesale basis, but rather it is allocated among relevant knowledge areas. Records are kept to show the patterns of advising and instruction that were used and who used them. All of these procedures are virtually absent in the quickie degree machinery of the diploma mill.

Individuals may acquire learning from work or life experiences outside of school or college classrooms. Such learning is of two basic types: (1) formal classroom or sponsored learning, usually in the form of courses or structured formal instruction offered by businesses, government agencies, labor unions, professional or voluntary associations and the military and (2) learning acquired on an individual basis through work experience, travel, reading, or self-study. By systematic assessment of either type of learning, colleges and universities may determine whether any of it is of college level and of a type applicable toward a college degree. Such learning must be documented against postsecondary education standards and must be assessed under appropriate academic protocols. Third party assessments (which are not the same as accreditation), such as those provided by ACE, are frequently required by colleges and universities for programs offered by sponsors other than postsecondary education institutions. According to a 1986 survey by ACE of a representative national sample, nearly all American colleges and universities (97 percent) have policies permitting the acceptance of credit for learning acquired in noncollegiate settings. Guidelines to assist in the process are offered in the American Council on Education's "Model Policy on Awarding Credit for Extrainstitutional Learning."

One of the authors of this volume has some direct experience with the concept of "life experience credit" as interpreted in a typical diploma mill transaction. After writing for information from the University of Beverly Hills, a legally authorized California institution, he was called at home around dinner time by a university employee who was doing a bit of recruiting. Was he interested in a University of Beverly Hills degree? If so, he might be interested in their "rough transcript" evaluation service. In return for a $50 fee, and completion of an "Assessment Evaluation Form," a determination would be made to see whether life experience credit might be a real possibility.

Within days, the completed form was on its way along with the required fee of $50. It contained the usual personal, educational, and employment data. A section on "goals and objectives" specified information about degree intentions as to major, reason for desiring a degree, and so forth. The completed form was both sides of one sheet of paper. As filled out, the form was accurate—up to a point. The "applicant" simply dropped the last twenty years from his resume. No longer was he a Washington-based higher education association executive and holder of the Ph.D. Instead, he reverted to an earlier incarnation as editor of a trade magazine in a midwestern city who held only a bachelor of arts degree.

In a cover letter, he indicated that as a professional editor, he was interested in a master's degree in journalism. He noted, however, that the University of Beverly Hills did not offer a journalism degree. Was this correct? If so, would it be possible to convert the master's degree in business communication or the master's degree in public relations to a journalism degree?

Also, was it true, as the person making the telephone call had said, that the university did not have accreditation because it was a "correspondence school?" Correspondence schools, he had been told during a telephone conversation with the recruiter, "were not eligible for accreditation." Rather, they were simply authorized to operate by the state government. (This statement by the organization's representative is not true.) He also wanted to know how the program would work. Would it be done entirely by correspondence? Would there be classes to attend if he could get to California for a week or two at times?

At the bottom of the completed Assessment Evaluation Form was a statement providing for signature by the applicant that the statements provided on the form were "true and accurate." Born and bred a Calvinist, he left this signature line blank.

The absence of his signature was no more of a hurdle than the absence of substance in the work experience category. In a follow-up phone call, the friendly voice from Beverly Hills was reassuring. No, they hadn't previously offered a journalism master's degree, but they were "revising their catalog" and soon would have one, just in time for his enrollment. It was their experience that "people want degrees fast. And the degrees are so extensive—we can confer degrees based on practically anything if the person has work experience in it. For example, suppose a policeman wants to turn exterminator, but he needs a degree in entomology or something like that. To get a license he needs a degree and apprenticeship. You know how it works—the subtleties."

However, the two members of the faculty review team who were to review the form had the flu, but, it had been determined, when they recovered, they would need a copy of the publication for which the applicant had served as editor in order to pass judgment on his request for work experience credit.

This request presented an unforeseen hurdle. A check in the attic revealed that the applicant did in fact have copies of every issue during his tenure as editor and earlier as associate editor. However, these issues were packaged in bound volumes. There were a few loose issues for the months immediately succeeding his resignation as editor, but his name appeared on these as "consulting editor" rather than editor. And there is a vast difference between the two, as anyone familiar with the publishing business would know. Making the best of the situation, he simply forwarded one of the twenty-year-old issues without comment.

After receiving this material, the folks at the University of Beverly Hills knew that the applicant for their rough transcript service was not shown as editor of the publication submitted in "proof" of his responsibilities as editor. They knew the publication was twenty years old, not contemporary and that the magazine was not located in the Washington area as had been implied. Also, they knew that the applicant had not certified that his statements on the form were true and accurate.

None of this made any difference, for the next letter, which came from the University of Beverly Hills "faculty advisor," extended congratulations on "provisional acceptance" to the external degree program. The Faculty Admissions Committee had "personally reviewed" the admissions materials and had recommended that "maximum academic credit be awarded to you for your career and life experiences. . . . It should take you no longer than six months to complete your program in total." It would not be necessary to spend any time in California.

The short time-frame was understandable since the "official transcript" that accompanied the letter showed no less than thirty credits had been granted for prior work experience on the magazine: five credits each in editing, publications, magazine journalism, public relations techniques, specialized reporting, and mass communication/popular culture.

To be sure, something called a "Final Project" to earn the remaining fifteen credits would have to be completed, but the university would be sending a "detailed set of guidelines" for doing this. The "Final Phase" itself (apparently in reference to a master's thesis) shouldn't take long, certainly "no longer than fifty hours to complete." Also, the faculty couldn't be nicer about the arrangements. The final project could be based "in part on reading you have already done in the past, as well as new reading which you may want to do. And again, remember that you may either choose the books yourself, or receive recommendations from our faculty."

Finally, the applicant was admonished to return all materials promptly "so that your projected graduation date of no longer than six months can be achieved."

The cost for this master's degree in journalism, which had not been mentioned in the institutional catalog, was $2,650 plus a graduation fee of $125. The application fee of $50 had, of course, been paid already. Since his funds were limited, the applicant did not proceed further, and Beverly Hills lost the chance to turn out still another graduate.

In fairness, it should be noted that the University of Beverly Hills closed as of December 1, 1986, an apparent casualty of the new California statutes regarding institutional authorization. However, thousands of persons must have graduated with degrees from legally authorized California-based institutions that pose requirements no more stringent than those described.

External Degree

An external (or extended) degree is one granted to an individual who has successfully completed an organized academic program specified by an educational institution or devised by the individual in consultation with institution faculty and accepted by the institution. Learning for the degree may be largely accomplished by means other than traditional, campus-based, classroom, residential study and might include independent reading, correspondence study, preparation of papers submitted to faculty for criticism, use of programmed instruction and computer and television media, as well as contract learning. Basically, an external degree is not a new type of degree in its content, but rather a degree that may be completed by nontraditional means.

Diploma mills advertise and award so-called external degrees practically on a mail order basis—conveniently overlooking the necessity to back up an external degree with a solid resource base. In legitimate external degree programs, the absence of regular class attendance is counterbalanced by the addition of other methods and resources, for example, media, mentors, agreements with employers, weekend seminars, and the like.

Evaluation of Formal Training

Diploma mills are casual, to say the least, about their awards of credit for formal training obtained under sponsorship other than that of a college or university. There is no excuse for such sloppy behavior because a number of tools are available now for evaluating such training or education programs. These are: (1) *ACE Guide to the Evaluation of Educational Experiences in the Armed Services,* (2) *ACE National Guide to Educational Credit for Training Programs,* and (3) the University of the State of New York *College Credit Recommendations.* In addition, qualified faculty members or others can evaluate occupational licenses or certification and can conduct hands-on evaluation of demonstrated student competencies to determine the college-level learning that has been acquired.

All of these resources and methods, used by well-qualified personnel and administered under appropriate academic protocols, are being applied by traditional American colleges and universities in awarding credit for learning attained through formal but noncollegiate sponsored education and training.

Portfolio Development

Another method of identifying and documenting prior experiential learning—and one frequently abused by diploma mills—is portfolio development. In applying for possible award of credit, a student assembles a portfolio or file of information about past experiences and accomplishments that may have resulted in college-level learning. With proper guidance, the student is helped to identify those activities resulting in learning that can be stated as educational outcomes or curriculum-relevant "competencies." The learning presented by the student is then carefully evaluated by the institution's faculty and/or assessors. In many cases, academic credit toward a degree can be awarded as the student enters a degree program.

The legitimate portfolio technique is characterized by detail and thoroughness by both student and faculty. Guidelines for academically sound programs of portfolio development are offered by the Council for Adult and Experiential Learning (CAEL) (Willingham, 1977).

Credit by Examination

One way of documenting college-level learning acquired outside postsecondary-level education institutions is by using nationally standardized or institutional, faculty-made examinations. Some 93 percent of American higher education institutions use such examinations according to an ACE study done in 1986 (Hexter and Andersen, 1986, p. vi). Institutions may use results of examinations in awarding credit toward a degree or waiving required courses.

Many suitable examinations are currently available for institutional credit-by-examination programs. Probably the most widely recognized series of such tests is the College Board's College-Level Examination Program (CLEP). Other examinations used to award credit include those of the State of New York Regents College Degrees and Examinations, the Defense Activity for Non-Traditional Education Support (DANTES), and the examinations developed by the American Chemical Society, the California State Colleges and Universities, the American College Testing Proficiency Examination Program (ACT PEP), and other education organizations. Most are designed to gauge comprehension of subject matter corresponding to a single college course; some are more general in scope. Department challenge examinations and faculty end-of-course examinations may also be used.

ACE publishes a *Guide To Educational Credit by Examination* (Whitney and Malizio, 1987). Users of this guide find an at-a-glance resource for all examinations evaluated and recommended by ACE as reliable and valid for use in awarding college credit. A wide variety of examinations are included in the *Guide*, such as those used by the Institute for Certification of Computer Professionals (ICCP) and the National Institute for Automotive Service Excellence, which were added in a 1987 supplement.

Contract Learning

Learning contracts are written agreements between an instructor and a student under which both parties set forth their joint understanding of the terms and conditions of a learning project. Such agreements ordinarily include statements of what is to be learned, how it will be learned, what resources will be used, evidence of learning that will be presented, date of completion, and who will assess whether the learning has been accomplished. Such contracts are being used increasingly in traditional classroom-based study, as well as in nontraditional programs designed for people having adult responsibilities.

Competency-Based Curricula

Mature adults entering a degree program are frequently found to possess significant and degree-relevant college-level learning derived from their work and life experiences. Such learning does not tend to be neatly organized to exactly match college courses, however. Competency-based curricula have been developed as a way of allowing credit for prior college-level learning, while at the same time allowing identification of those learning competencies that must still be acquired before a degree can be awarded. Competencies are basically units or modules of learning that are generally narrower in scope than traditional courses. A typical course, for example, may consist of eight basic competencies. If an incoming student is found to have already mastered five of these, he or she will be given credit for these five competencies and be required to acquire the three others. This new learning may be undertaken by enrolling in only part of the full course. Or perhaps the remaining competencies can be acquired via an independent or semi-independent learning activity agreed upon by the student and the faculty member.

Correspondence Study

Because it is hardly a new idea, correspondence study is not always thought of as an instrument of nontraditional higher education. But independent study—facilitated by correspondence with a faculty member at the sponsoring institution—is a vital ingredient in most nontraditional programs. In a soundly conceived program, lesson materials are prepared in a sequential and logical order. As students complete lessons, they send them to the institutional sponsor for correction, comment, subject matter guidance, and grading by a qualified instructor. In recent years, electronic technology has begun to play a significant role in such exchanges, giving an entirely new meaning to the word "correspondence."

Diploma mills have long been a thorn in the side of legitimate institutions offering correspondence instruction. Lessons submitted to them, if reviewed and graded at all, are reviewed by persons who may not have the needed subject-matter expertise. Sometimes a kind of pseudo feedback is arranged so that naive or unwary students are kept on the rolls, paying fees, for months, even years. This kind of corruption continues unabated into the present era.

As diploma mills bludgeon their way through the exper-
imental and often fragile world of nontraditional education,
they create enormous problems of credibility for nontraditional programs that are soundly conceived and implemented.
The chief victim of diploma mill activity in America may, in
fact, be nontraditional programs of study and nontraditional
students at institutions of higher education accredited by an
agency recognized by the COPA. As diploma mills ignore or
abuse legitimate procedures, the entire practice of nontraditional education may be called into question.

Two myths about nontraditional learning in higher education settings have been set out and nourished by diploma
mill operators and their allies. The first myth is that generally
recognized colleges and universities do not have programs
that really serve the needs of mature adults who have work
and family responsibilities. The second is that a commitment
to nontraditional learning is what disqualifies the diploma mill
from accreditation. Neither of these statements is true.

In advertising their wares and justifying their existence,
diploma mills are apt to cite the reluctance of traditional institutions and accrediting bodies to meet the needs of adult
and part-time students. There is some truth to this charge.
A few institutions, as is their prerogative, do not consider
programs serving adults to be within their current missions.
Most American colleges and universities do wish to attract
today's more mature students, but some have been shamefully
remiss in failing to adapt (or even consider adapting) their
programs to meet the needs of those students.

However, this charge is not true across the board. A
large number of respected colleges and universities have taken
major steps toward tailoring their programs to meet the needs
of adult learners. Also, even institutions that resisted such
change in the past have taken decidedly different tacks in
recent years. This trend can be documented by the popularity
of workshops on adapting programs to better serve adult
learners that have been conducted by such sponsors as ACE's
Commission on Higher Education and the Adult Learner, the
College Board, and Harvard University.

Accrediting agencies, too, are looking to their responsibilities to the new breed of adult students. COPA's 1986 self-study advisory panel encouraged member accrediting bodies to "review and modify, as appropriate, standards relative to part-time students, adult and continuing education, and continuing education as a part of professional and personal renewal." It also urged that provisions for access to postsecondary education not be "overlooked in the concern for quality improvement" (COPA, 1986, p. 11).

Consideration of the needs of part-time students, along with issues relating to continuing education, equity, and access were explicitly cited as desirable for inclusion "on the agenda for any national conference on quality improvement sponsored by COPA or other national organizations." While much work in this area remains to be done, main-line postsecondary education institutions are attending to the learning concerns of adult students.

Does this trend extend to the relatively conservative world of graduate programs? In 1977, the Council of Graduate Schools in the United States published a policy paper on "Non-Residential Graduate Degree Programs." While believing strongly that development of external degree programs was "an important trend in American higher education" and that the "healthy growth of such programs" should be encouraged and supported by the Council, the authors of the paper took note of "questions . . . regarding the quality of courses and programs" (Council of Graduate Schools, 1977).

Taking up this challenge to the graduate community, John Harris, William E. Troutt, and Grover J. Andrews examined the American doctorate in the context of new patterns in higher education. While not minimizing the problems involved, they found "no basis for an accrediting body to limit member institutions from considering a nontraditional approach to any doctoral program" and no cause either "for refusing to consider applying institutions because they offer the Ph.D. nontraditionally. Nothing suggests the Ph.D. should be uniquely reserved for traditional institutions and programs" (Harris, Troutt, and Andrews, 1980, p. 19).

Among other misstatements of fact given currency by representatives of diploma mills is that an institution offering

courses by correspondence only or by means other than traditional class-based study is not eligible for accreditation. This
is untrue. A number of institutions accredited by COPA-recognized bodies do not even have campus facilities. They *do*
have resources for assessing and granting credit for prior
college-level learning by means of credit by examination, portfolio development, and similar academic mechanisms. They
also have appropriate instructional or related support services
or access to such resources under formal agreements with
other agencies and institutions.

The National Home Study Council, a COPA-recognized
accrediting agency, offers accreditation to institutions that
deliver courses by correspondence study. The Accrediting
Commission of the Council currently accredits eight degree-
granting institutions offering associate or baccalaureate degrees in such areas as business management, accounting, Bi-
ble-theology, travel and tourism, electronics, and engineering
technology.

In addition, about seventy colleges and universities accredited by regional accrediting bodies offer academic courses
for credit via correspondence study. More than 12,000 courses
in more than 1,000 subject areas (most of them at the undergraduate level) are offered.

It is even possible to earn a degree entirely by examination. Agencies in four states, New York, New Jersey, Illinois, and Connecticut, are organized solely for the purpose
of enabling individuals to demonstrate their acquisition of college-level learning by passing examinations. These are the
Regents College Degrees and Examinations of New York
State, Thomas A. Edison State College in New Jersey, the
Board of Governors Bachelor of Arts Degree Program in Illinois, and Charter Oak College/Board for State Academic
Awards in Connecticut.

The Commission on Institutions of Higher Education of
the New England Association of Schools and Colleges specifies
in its *Handbook of Accreditation* that procedures in nontraditional programs "should encourage innovative and imaginative approaches to providing quality education whether in
new institutions or in those already accredited." The Com-

mission further acknowledges that at the present early stage in development of nontraditional degree programs, "the principles, policies, and procedures specified for accreditation must be flexible and of an interim nature." The Commission accordingly states that its own statement of policies and principles regarding nontraditional study should be considered as "tentative and interim" (New England Association, 1983, p. 100).

The Accrediting Commission for Senior Colleges and Universities of the Western Association of Schools and Colleges (WASC) has also taken a positive, yet cautious, approach. In its *Handbook of Accreditation*, the Commission explicitly recognizes that "undergraduate learning takes place in a variety of ways and settings and covers a broad spectrum of ages and experience." It further recognizes that "college-level learning, judged by recognized academic criteria, but based on experiences other than those that occur in an academic setting, may be educationally creditable."

However, the Commission notes that a sound program for evaluation of prior experiential learning cannot be undertaken casually. The institution needs to have "a well-defined philosophy regarding the awarding of credit, a clear statement of evaluation procedures, and a definitive plan to evaluate the amount of academic credit to be awarded" (Western Association, 1982, p. 114).

Some state governments have also taken action to control academic banditry that parades as nontraditional education. Ohio, for example, strictly enforces its law requiring authorization from the Ohio Board of Regents for any postsecondary education institution doing business in the state. Moreover, state statutes require that special authorization is necessary when half or more of a degree program or degree program major is offered at a location removed from the central campus—a stricture specified for Ohio's domestic institutions also.

Ohio reviews all academic programming against the following criteria: institutional mission and purpose, academic planning, academic control systems, faculty, curriculum, and resources and support services. An organization must give added assurance that off-campus programs meet all of these criteria, with particular emphasis on the adequacy of resources and services available to students at off-campus locations (e.g., access to collegiate-level library resources, provision of student support services, etc).

It is instructive to review Ohio's method for applying criteria to within-state, off-campus programming by its own institutions. (Because of staff limitation the Board of Regents does not monitor out-of-state or international off-campus programs sponsored by its own institutions.) Patricia Skinner, former Director of Continuing Education and Certificates of Authorization for the Ohio Board of Regents, cites both positive and "problematic" characteristics of off-campus programs that have been evaluated over a five-year period as shown in the following chart (Skinner, 1987a).

EVALUATION OF CHARACTERISTICS OF
OFF-CAMPUS PROGRAMS

Positive Characteristics	Problematic Characteristics
Mission/Purpose	
Off-campus program consistent with institutional mission and resources	No comparable central campus program; lack of institutional commitment and resources; primary purpose income generation
Academic Planning	
Sufficient academic planning conducted prior to initiation of each off-campus program	Program developed by administration and/or faculty in immediate response to perceived need, without sufficient academic planning
Academic Control	
Design, conduct, and evaluation of off-campus activities under direct and continuous control of sponsoring institution's established processes	Lack of site supervision and coordination of part-time faculty; inadequate system of faculty and student evaluations; lack of provisions for advising, counseling, and admissions control

EVALUATION OF CHARACTERISTICS OF
OFF-CAMPUS PROGRAMS (*continued*)

Positive Characteristics	Problematic Characteristics
Curriculum	
Curriculum of off-campus program comparable to central campus counterpart	No admissions standards; lack of prerequisites; courses substituted due to lack of facilities or resources; acceptance of credit from other institutions inconsistent with generally accepted practices; course content and rigor in variance with central campus program
Faculty	
Sufficient number of qualified full- and part-time faculty members with necessary commitment and involvement in the program	Lack of available full-time central faculty members; marginally qualified part-time faculty members utilized with little or no supervision from central campus
Resources/Supporting Services	
Facilities and supporting services appropriate to collegiate level instruction; access provided to needed library services, laboratories, and computer facilities; contractual agreements made with all cooperating institutions to assure continuity for students	Facilities inappropriate for collegiate level instruction; students left to find own resources; no academic advising or other student support services

Reliable guides to accredited institutions offering nontraditional programs do exist. The *Guide to External Degree Programs in the United States*, edited by Eugene Sullivan, contains listings of programs at both the undergraduate and graduate levels that are designed to meet the needs of working persons and other part-time students. Another reliable guide is the American Association of Collegiate Registrars and Admissions Officers' (AACRAO) *Directory of Colleges and Universities with Non-traditional Educational Programs/Systems/Practices* published in 1987.

6
Dipscam: Diploma Mills and the FBI

Given the objective of issuing worthless degrees and a willingness to risk violation of federal laws, how does one proceed? An infinite number of imaginative variations on the diploma mill theme exist, ranging from the simple printing of diplomas to the creation of massive empires that provide not only degrees, but a host of other related accessories. However, there are substantial hazards in these activities because they may attract the sharp and roving eyes of the Federal Bureau of Investigation (FBI).

The American public can rest assured about the quality and intensity of FBI efforts to stamp out illegal diploma mills. From its regional office in Charlotte, North Carolina, the FBI directs its diploma scam operation—Dipscam—which targets diploma mill operations that may be in violation of federal laws concerning mail and wire fraud. Special agent Otho Allen Ezell, Jr., and others working with him are old hands at posing as students who want diploma mill degrees. Ezell may, in fact, be the world's most credentialed man holding, at last count, some thirty-seven degrees from thirty-three fraudulent colleges and universities. Fifteen such degrees have been garnered by other agents.

Acquiring hard evidence has paid off. Since 1981, the FBI has executed ten search warrants in thirty-nine so-called schools and related businesses in South Carolina, New York, California, Oregon, Arkansas, Florida, Tennessee, and Ohio. To date, these efforts have resulted in nineteen individuals being convicted for diploma mill-related fraud. Sentences ranging from incarceration to community service have been meted out by the courts. As of December 11, 1985, the FBI had identified more than 7,000 individuals living in the United States who possessed degrees from these sham institutions (U.S. Congress, House, p. 100).

Nature of the Fraud

Illegal diploma mills include those organizations that (1) issue diplomas or related documents of virtually nonexistent colleges or universities, or (2) forge diplomas or other related documents of legitimate colleges or universities. (However unscrupulous, it is not necessarily a violation of *federal* laws to grant degrees in return for educational activity that is less demanding than that traditionally associated with the awarding of postsecondary degrees by colleges and universities in the United States.)

Along with transcripts of student academic records, diplomas are the most important official documents issued by American colleges and universities. A diploma signifies that an individual has satisfied requirements for a degree. Typically, diplomas specify the major field of study and the degree earned. The date the degree was awarded and the school or college faculty responsible for awarding the degree also appear, along with any academic honors. Diplomas are customarily signed by the president, the dean, the chairman of the board of regents or trustees, and the institution's registrar.

In the United States, diplomas are seldom submitted as

direct evidence of educational attainment by persons seeking employment, entry to other higher education institutions, or for professional certification or licensing. Instead, transcripts usually serve this purpose. In most foreign nations, however, the opposite is true—the diploma is presented as evidence. This fact makes American diplomas and transcripts alike especially vulnerable to abuse in foreign countries.

In recent times, diplomas issued by legitimate American universities have become the vehicles for serious fraud when their diplomas are duplicated by counterfeiters calling themselves "diploma replacement services." The extent of these operations has been a source of great shock to college and university registrars, according to Bruce Shutt, Associate Vice President for Student Affairs and Registrar of the University of Georgia, in testimony before the Subcommittee on Health and Long-Term Care of the U.S. House of Representatives Select Committee on Aging. Shutt was appearing as President (1985–86) of the American Association of Collegiate Registrars and Admissions Officers (AACRAO) (U.S. Congress, House, 11 December 1985, p. 80).

Examples of Fraud

One clearly illegal practice is the forging or "replacing" of diplomas from legitimate universities. In a prepared statement before the Subcommittee, Anthony E. Daniels, Inspector-Deputy Assistant Director in the Criminal Investigative Division of the FBI, described the degree replacement service as the "easiest scam of all." An example is the Alumni Arts of Grants Pass, Oregon, which ran advertisements for its services in various publications. It offered to sell a replacement degree for $39.95. If the lost degree was not in stock, there was an additional $25 "custom order" fee.

Beginning in December of 1982 and extending through June of 1984, this organization operated as a small business from the home of its sole proprietor. The gross revenue during this time was about $100,000. Some 33,000 degrees and certificates for more than 330 legitimate educational institutions in the United States, Canada, and England were printed.

Some 32,000 blank degree forms were seized during the ex-
ecution of a search warrant. The FBI also found that Alumni
Arts had sold about 2,300 degrees and certificates—all without
the knowledge of institutions who were purported to have
issued the documents.

Among the first to be snared in the FBI's Dipscam net
were Anthony James Geruntino and James Robert Caffey
who, with five others, were indicted in 1985 on charges brought
by a federal grand jury. Working on evidence provided by
the FBI Office in Charlotte, North Carolina, the grand jury
charged that the group

> unlawfully, knowingly, and willfully devised and intended to
> devise a scheme and artifice to defraud [citizens] of their ex-
> pectation of properly educated, competent, appropriately trained
> and tested, and otherwise qualified, legal, educational, psy-
> chological, engineering, business, and health consultation and
> assistance from trained persons and professionals purportedly
> having received degrees, certificates, diplomas, and tran-
> scripts from legitimate, accredited and qualified institutions
> with legitimate authority to provide such training and confer
> such degrees. (U.S. vs. Geruntino et al., p. 2)

In short, they operated diploma mills and related businesses.

The grand jury found this endeavor to be quite a "scheme
and artifice." For one thing, the project required inventive-
ness and organizational skill to create names for and launch
twenty-two bogus colleges, universities, accrediting entities,
professional consulting services, and related organizations in
a number of states. The group (not all of whom were involved
in every activity or involved to the same degree) used the
following names: Northwestern College of Allied Science, National College, St. Paul Seminary, South Union Graduate
School, National College of Arts and Sciences, American
Western University, and Southwestern University. It was no
accident that some of these names duplicate or nearly duplicate the names of legitimate institutions. All were presented
as legitimate, bonafide educational institutions empowered to
confer degrees and diplomas in legal, psychological, engineering, educational, health, and other fields. A few "marginal

requirements" might be specified (possibly including a thesis). But work demonstrating college-level academic achievement was not required before the degree or diploma was conferred.

Accreditation? No problem. In the absence of approval by agencies recognized by the Council on Postsecondary Accreditation (COPA), the team used homemade organizations under the names of the National Association of Open Campus Colleges and Mid-Western States Accrediting Agency (also known as the Mid-Western Accrediting Agency, Midwest Accrediting Agency, and Mid-West Accrediting Association).

For nearly five years, one of the group, Anthony Geruntino, engaged in the business of "expediting" the delivery of college degrees. Through a company called Vocational Guidance, Inc., in Columbus, Ohio, he placed advertisements in numerous publications such as *Popular Mechanics*, *Popular Science*, *Psychology Today*, and the *National Enquirer*. Client contact was typically arranged via mail. The advertisements proclaimed that students could get Southwestern University degrees—"inexpensive and fast"—based on their life experience.

While his home base was Ohio, Geruntino was careful not to award degrees there since the state had strict laws governing the authorization of private postsecondary education institutions. Such laws included a requirement that there be evidence of planned curricula and faculty. Because of less stringent authorization standards in Missouri and other states, the paper degrees were awarded there.

Southwestern University was "incorporated" in Arizona because at that time Arizona had weak laws governing the activities of private postsecondary academic institutions. Therefore Geruntino had no state-mandated guidelines to meet, no on-site inspection requirements, no licensing or verification procedures for corporate officers or faculty members, no required annual disclosure statements, and no state agency assigned as a watchdog.

In January of 1985, Arizona passed a law greatly strengthening its statutes governing authorization and operation of academic institutions. It became riskier for Geruntino to continue awarding degrees there. According to the

FBI, Geruntino then arranged for mail delivered at Tucson to be picked up by a secretarial service and forwarded un-opened to his office in Columbus, Ohio.

What did the Geruntino–Caffey group offer the holders of its diplomas? Promises. Promises. Promises. Some thirty-seven in all—and none of them kept in the view of the grand jury. For example, the American Western University's "spe-cial evaluation review of the resume (credentials)" of an ap-plicant was represented as "equivalent to the standard college equivalency tests offered by most traditional colleges through-out the world." The grand jury was not impressed with Amer-ican Western's procedure specifying that "all diplomas would be dated on the Friday following the . . . applicant's special evaluation date approval." An applicant might, however, re-quest a special date "if he felt his qualifications for the degree were completed in a prior year." There were limits, however, to American Western's generosity in awarding degrees. No date prior to 1956 could be selected as the date of the degree, since that was "the founding year of the parent body of the University."

How much did the degrees cost? A credential suited for any pocketbook could be obtained. According to the grand jury record, only $51 would buy a bachelor's, master's, or doctoral degree from Northwestern College of Allied Science ("Under the Direction of Disciples of Truth, Inc.") if the trans-action was processed by James Caffey, the original proprietor. However, the same institution charged $290 for a bachelor's degree, $340 for a master's degree, and $590 for a doctorate when Caffey gave Geruntino permission to award its degrees. For $200 one could have "any religious degree"—and, for an additional $50, an "ordination" for good measure. For $20, a transcript would arrive in your mailbox. Northwestern Col-lege of Allied Science was ever-mindful, too, of the needs of those degree candidates "who have neglected to secure a High School Diploma." The National Research Institute, a division of the college, would step in with a "special evaluation," in return for $45, for an equivalency certificate (U.S. vs. Ger-untino, et al., 6 February 1985).

Southwestern University apparently catered to a more

affluent group of customers than did Northwestern College of Allied Science. If Southwestern's clients were upwardly mobile, so were its prices. At one time, a bachelor's degree from Southwestern cost $575, a master's degree was $795, and the doctorate was $1,050. These prices were eventually raised to $985, $1,135, and $1,450 respectively. There was good news for quantity purchasers at American Western University—anyone purchasing more than one "degree evaluation" at a time could get a hefty 25 percent discount.

Running a diploma mill empire takes more than just a few colleges and universities with supporting accrediting and career placement entities. Names for sponsoring organizations are also needed, as are names suggesting the presence of academic support services, alumni associations, financial consultants, even businesses. At various times the group used the names Disciples of Truth, Incorporated, Northwestern Corporate Finance (Center), American Western Financial Corporation, Northwestern Alumni Association, American Western Alumni Association, National Evaluation Center, American Western Evaluation Center, Southwestern Program Information, and Joel Jewelry as they did business (U.S. vs. Geruntino, et al., 6 February 1985).

Members of the indicted combine made a serious mistake when they made telephone calls and rented postal boxes in Tulsa, Oklahoma; Springfield, Missouri; Columbus, Ohio; and other U.S. cities to send and receive messages for their far-flung empire (U.S. vs. Geruntino, et al., 6 February 1985). Those actions initiated the FBI investigation, and their subsequent presentation of charges to the North Carolina grand jury.

The FBI's actions against diploma mill operators are perhaps typified by their pursuit of Anthony Geruntino. On April 15, 1982, Geruntino made (one of several) fatal errors when he awarded a master's degree in business administration from Southwestern University to an undercover FBI agent at a cost of $510. The same agent received a second M.B.A. degree from one of Geruntino's employees for $830. Both degrees were accompanied by transcripts which reflected numerous courses and grades, even though no course work was assigned or completed, nor was any other work required. The FBI agent also toured the Columbus office (U.S. Congress, House, 11 December 1985, pp. 49–52).

On October 13, 1982, the FBI executed a search warrant and seized records and student files at both Tucson and Columbus. These documents include the names of graduates of Southwestern University, "alumni records" of American Western University, and users of the vocational guidance and placement services (U.S. Congress, House, 11 December 1985, pp. 49–52).

During late 1984, just prior to new legislation concerning authorization of educational institutions becoming effective in Arizona, Geruntino moved Southwestern University to St. George, Utah, a state with notoriously weak authorization laws. But the FBI was not far behind. Geruntino was arrested on February 6, 1985, in St. George though he remained free on bond. Decidedly displeased with this state of affairs, officials in St. George rescinded Geruntino's license to do business in the city. According to FBI agent Otho Allen Ezell, Geruntino then moved to Salt Lake City and even with charges pending against him, he managed to "graduate" a class of seventy-five students by mid-April with no interference from Utah state authorities.

In the meantime, the FBI was not sitting by idly. It put its case before a federal grand jury in the Western District of North Carolina at Charlotte. On February 7, 1985, the jury returned a 31-count indictment charging Geruntino and his cohorts with wire and mail fraud, conspiracy, and aiding and abetting in their operation of diploma mills and associated organizations since February 10, 1980 (U.S. vs. Geruntino, et al., 6 February 1985).

Four of those indicted, including Geruntino, pleaded guilty to the grand jury charges. On May 22, 1985, Geruntino appeared in the U.S. District Court at Charlotte and entered guilty pleas to violations of both fraud by wire and mail. On July 8, he was sentenced to five years in prison and fined $5,000.

In the latest phase of its Dipscam operation, the FBI on December 3, 1986, was successful in getting a federal grand jury in Charlotte, North Carolina, to return a 29-count indictment charging Norman Bradley Fowler, his brother, mother, two sisters, and two others with conspiracy, aiding and abetting, and mail fraud in their operation of numerous diploma mills and/or fictional accrediting entities in Switzerland, Belgium, France, England, The Netherlands, and West Germany. These individuals, who based their operations in Chicago and Los Angeles, utilized various private mail-receiving facilities and bank accounts.

Degrees sold ranged from associate through the doctorate with accompanying transcripts. The range in cost was $365 to $740, with both backdating and verification to employers and other educational institutions also available. Names used in these endeavors were Roosevelt University, Cromwell University, Lafayette University, and DePaul University. Among the 110 witnesses called to testify at the subsequent trial were representatives of the legitimate DePaul, Loyola, and Roosevelt Universities (all located in Illinois).

On October 2, 1987, at the conclusion of the government's presentation of evidence, the presiding judge dismissed all charges against two of the defendents. On October 5, the jury returned guilty verdicts on all twenty-seven counts on the remaining five defendants (including Norman Fowler). The judge sentenced these individuals to prison terms ranging from two to seven years (Ezell interview, 1987).

7
Diploma Mills and Fraudulent Occupational Licensure: Findings of the U.S. House of Representatives Select Committee on Aging

An unusual opportunity to look inside the unsavory world of diploma mills and phony credentials was provided when the U.S. House of Representatives Select Committee on Aging began its investigation of fraud against the elderly. In hearings held by the Committee's Subcommittees on Health and

Long-Term Care chaired by Rep. Claude Pepper (D-Florida) and Housing and Consumer Interests chaired by Rep. Don Bonker (D-Washington), a parade of witnesses helped document the scope and nature of America's diploma mill problem. The investigation began with a focus on credential fraud affecting health care concerns, but was broadened when it became evident that the true dimensions of the problem were more pervasive.

In December 1984, the Pepper Subcommittee held a hearing on fraudulent medical credentials. While stating that "many excellent foreign medical schools" exist, the Subcommittee felt it had "every reason to question the quality of medical education obtained by the majority of American students educated abroad." Even more troubling was the Subcommittee finding that for many years, the United States had inadvertently allowed some of its citizens to practice medicine with "doctored" credentials, primarily bearing the names of small foreign medical schools of questionable quality. These same individuals had been allowed to receive medical licenses without displaying the same level of medical knowledge and clinical competence as graduates of American medical schools. It was also discovered that most state and federal agencies had relatively lax systems for checking the credentials of graduates of foreign medical schools (U.S. Congress, House, 7 December 1984, p. 2). (Subcommittee members later influenced the amending of the Higher Education Act so that new criteria can be applied to foreign medical school graduates seeking guaranteed student loans.)

Following its December 1984 hearing with its findings, the Pepper Subcommittee received "numerous letters and calls from all over the United States" regarding experiences with phony practitioners. Such problems were chronicled "all across the professional spectrum," not just the medical specialties (U.S. Congress, House, 11 December 1985, p. 2).

The Subcommittee went to work in earnest. Its staff conducted a review of all credential fraud case histories received either directly or by request from state licensing boards and 250 college and university registrars. It reviewed books, periodicals, and newspaper articles relating to credentialing abuses for the previous five years. It also requested and obtained "details" sent to the Subcommittee from the U.S. Postal Inspection Service, one of the federal agencies vested with primary enforcement authority over the mail fraud statutes. Subcommittee staffers also responded to numerous advertisements in hundreds of publications to determine firsthand whether the advertisements lived up to the promises made.

To simulate the problems it was addressing, the Subcommittee even set up its own "university" which it called "Capitol Institute of Advanced Education." Following step-by-step instructions in the guide provided by the District of Columbia government's Corporation Division, the Subcommittee staff drew up articles of incorporation for the institute in just one half hour meeting. The articles listed as Capitol's "campus" the address of one Subcommittee staff member's apartment, as its board of directors and incorporators three Subcommittee staff, and as its first objective to provide "educational opportunities" and "educational guidance" to professionals in the metropolitan Washington area. Two original copies of these articles along with a $42 fee were enough to launch Capitol Institute of Advanced Education as an incorporated business (U.S. Congress, House, 11 December 1985, pp. 135–136).

Incorporation was easy enough though authorization to award degrees under the District of Columbia's relatively strong laws was another matter. But authorization was a temporary hurdle. The Subcommittee learned that it could incorporate as a second university in a state which did not have strong laws regarding authorization to award degrees and that this would constitute "full compliance" with the laws in the District of Columbia. And so, for a fee of $50 a new "National University" was incorporated in Salt Lake City under the easy laws of the State of Utah. National University in Utah could grant degrees based on the recommendations of Capitol Institute of Advanced Education in Washington, D.C. (U.S. Congress, House, 11 December 1985, p. 136). All of this could be accomplished with no faculty, curriculum, or academic resources.

With its homemade universities, the Subcommittee could

have enjoyed quick success. It placed ads in a Washington paper and within a week's time had letters of inquiry from prospective students.

Other evidence of the ease with which degrees are obtainable came when the Subcommittee acquired a Ph.D. in psychology for its Chairman, Claude Pepper. The degree was dated November 23, 1985, and came from Union University which then operated legally in Los Angeles under California statutes. The price: $1,810 and submission of four book reports (on books entitled *The Power of Positive Thinking*, *Plain Speaking*, *Too Old, Too Sick, Too Bad*, and *Mental Health and the Elderly*) and a list of forty-four books read—all of this work being done and submitted by members of the Subcommittee staff. Upon receiving his diploma, the Chairman quipped, "I have always wanted to be Dr. Pepper" (U.S. Congress, House, 11 December 1985, p. 19).

The Subcommittee subsequently called upon the General Accounting Office (GAO) to conduct a study to determine, among other things, what the role of the federal government should be in curbing the "proliferation of ill-trained or fraudulent medical practitioners." In its report, submitted in October 1985, the GAO made three important statements on the problem: its essence was inadequate training of Americans studying medicine abroad; it was getting worse; and it needed to be corrected by government action. (U.S. Congress, House, 11 December 1985, p. 120). In convening the December 1985 hearing, the two subcommittees initiated a process aimed at correcting the problem.

Results of the investigations as contained in the 1984 and 1985 hearing records are disturbing. In their joint statement opening a hearing, Representatives Pepper and Bonker warned that "every American can have cause for concern in the search for a bonafide professional." What was termed "most shocking" to the two Congressmen was the finding of the Subcommittee on Health and Long-Term Care that so many older Americans are the target of medical fraud schemes. Although older Americans comprise about 11 percent of the nation's population, they account for about 60 percent of the victims of medical fraud, which costs the nation about $10 billion an-

Union University

207 North Broad Street

Los Angeles, California 90033

November 23, 1985

Mr. C.D. Pepper
9509 Burke Lake Road,
Burke, VA 22015

Dear Mr. Pepper,

The Graduation Committee is pleased to approve your degree and graduation status. Your oral defense of your subject, as you may know, was successful. Congratulations!

Upon receiving your "Candidate Checklist," I find that all requirements have been completed and your tuition is Paid in full .

Therefore, it gives Union University and myself personally great pleasure to inform you that you are approved to be awarded the degree of ___Doctor of Philosophy___ in ___Psychology___. We shall, of course, follow your wishes regarding participation in the Commencement Ceremony. You may accept your diploma at that time, ask that it be sent to you now, or arrange to come to the university to personally accept it.

Once again, it is my distinct honor to advise you of your success in achieving your earned degree. Union University is proud of graduates such as yourself and wishes you every success with your future. We look forward to your suggestions and support of our Alumni Association during the upcoming year.

Hardiest Congratulations,

Dr. Terry Suzuki
Director of External Program
Union University (JGB-K0001)

Union University is proud of its newest alumnus as of November 23, 1985. (Courtesy of Subcommittee on Health and Long-Term Care, Select Committee on Aging, U.S. House of Representatives.)

Rep. Claude Pepper (D-Florida) receives diploma from Representative Ron Wyden (D-Oregon), another member of the Subcommittee on Health and Long-Term Care of the Select Committee on Aging of the U.S. House of Representatives. At right is Representative Ralph Regula (R-Ohio), ranking minority member of the Subcommittee. (Courtesy of Subcommittee on Health and Long-Term Care, Select Committee on Aging, U.S. House of Representatives.)

nually. Spurred by this finding, the Subcommittee was moving to take a closer look at what it considered the most pervasive form of health fraud—the provision of medical care by unlicensed and unqualified people posing as doctors (U.S. Congress, House, 11 December 1985, p. 119).

The subcommittees learned that fraud is endemic and that the problem is increasing. They reported that some 500,000 Americans have secured credentials that are purchased, not earned. (According to Peter Reinecke, the Pepper Subcommittee's Director of Research, this figure includes 10,000 medical degrees plus estimates of phony degrees in other fields—all derived from FBI records.) In addition, the subcommittees reported, about 30 million Americans (one in three who are employed) may have been hired on the basis of a resume that was less than accurate with respect to credentials earned (U.S. Congress, House, 11 December 1985, p. 123).*

How many "checkbook doctors" exist? No one knows but the subcommittees estimated that "upward of 10,000 so-called doctors now in hospitals and private practice have obtained fraudulent or highly questionable medical credentials. One doctor in every fifty practices with false or questionable credentials" (U.S. Congress, House, 11 December 1985, pp. 119, 123).

The subcommittees found that Americans "continue to be receiving medical treatment from doctors who either stole or paid for their degrees, or stole or paid for a copy of an exam which had to be passed before they could practice." In July 1983, "3,000 to 4,000 of the 17,000 students who took the test for foreign medical graduates saw the answers in advance" (U.S. Congress, House, 11 December 1985, p. 119).

How much does a phony credential cost? Anywhere from $5 for an "outstanding service citation" to $28,000 for a medical degree with accompanying transcripts, diplomas, letters of recommendation, and employment verification services, according to the Subcommittee findings (U.S. Congress, House, 11 December 1985, p. 123).

Who are the victims of medical credential fraud? Employers are big losers when they hire or promote persons on the basis of false or worthless credentials. Patients and colleagues of ersatz doctors or other professionals are exploited

---

*Elaine Miller, President of Credential Check and Personnel Services, a verification service located in Farmington Hills, Michigan, reports slightly lower, though still appalling, figures. Approximately 20 percent of the credentials checked by her firm contain something untruthful about *academic* credentials. One of the most common practices is to claim a bachelor's degree in engineering while possessing only an associate degree in engineering technology.

and perhaps injured. So, too, are legitimate educational institutions offering degrees designed to meet the needs of
working adults.

Certainly the most dramatic witness called by the Pepper
Subcommittee was Pedro de Mesones. In August 1983, representatives of the Postal Inspection Service arrested Pedro
de Mesones of Alexandria, Virginia. Mr. de Mesones's arrest
followed an investigation into allegations that he was in the
business of arranging for the issuance of medical degrees from
two medical schools in the Caribbean.

The arrest and conviction of de Mesones and the attempt
to identify and locate the individuals who had purchased degrees from him led to one of the major scandals in the field
of contemporary medicine. As a result, investigations were
initiated in fifteen states. The process by which foreign medical school graduates are licensed in the United States and
the quality of education provided by these foreign medical
schools was brought into question. Several other brokers of
medical degrees were identified and put under investigation.

The Subcommittee report goes on to make it clear that
the de Mesones matter was "but the tip of the iceberg." Responsible federal, state, and private agencies had not shown
the ability to detect and screen impostors. Soberingly, federal
funds were thought to have "fueled the problem to a significant
degree" through educational loans (U.S. Congress, House, 7
December 1984, p. 7).

In a prepared statement before the Pepper Subcommittee, Pedro de Mesones, by then a resident of the Allenwood
Federal Correctional Center in Pennsylvania, spun out his
story (U.S. Congress, House, 7 December 1984, pp. 11–25).

The Case of Pedro de Mesones and Friends

For about three years, de Mesones said, he had been in
the business of "expediting" medical degrees through a company organized in the District of Columbia. Under the name
"Medical Education Placement, Inc.," he placed advertisements in papers such as the *New York Times* and the *Los
Angeles Times*, as well as in various professional journals.

The ads stated that students could obtain medical, Ph.D., and dental degrees through Medical Education Placement's services.

De Mesones might have avoided difficulties for himself had he been more inquisitive about the background of one prospective student who identified herself as Odette Bouchard. She was, in fact, an undercover agent of the U.S. Postal Inspection Service.

In order to become "Dr. Bouchard" she paid $16,500, and it was accordingly arranged that she graduate from one of the foreign medical schools having ties with de Mesones. There were no classes to attend and no hassle about getting transcripts and letters of reference. Bouchard did go to Santo Domingo, but only for the purpose of picking up her medical degree and transcript. It was this transcript that allowed the Postal Service law enforcement officials to close in and arrest de Mesones.

Diplomas, transcripts, and letters of reference were not the only services provided by de Mesones. He arranged for clinical placements and rotations in American schools in a conspiracy with Dr. Joseph McPike of Polk General Hospital in Florida. His cooperating medical schools in the Dominican Republic were *Universidad Centro de Estudios Technologicos (CETEC)* and *Universidad Centro de Investigacion, Formacion y Assistencia Social* (CIFAS).

De Mesones served 165 clients during his three years of business operations. About one hundred of them received transcripts showing they had fulfilled medical requirements at institutions they did not attend. Eventually, forty of his clients were certified by the Educational Commission for Foreign Medical Graduates. Thirteen obtained their medical licenses to practice and six more were working in hospital residency programs at the time of the Postal Inspection Service investigation.

The cost of doing business with de Mesones ranged from $5,225 to $26,000. His gross during the three and one-half year period was approximately $1.5 million though he got to keep only about $433,000 to $500,000 of this total; the rest went for "bribes and expenses."

Cartoonist Gary Trudeau periodically has fun with the Caribbean medical school scandal. (Copyright 1984 by G. B. Trudeau. Reprinted with permission of Universal Press Syndicate. All Rights Reserved.)

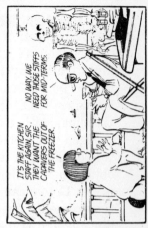

In its spring 1985 *Law Enforcement Report*, the U.S Postal Inspection Service chronicled what happened to some of de Mesones's would-be doctors. "As a result of a continuing investigation by Postal Inspectors, a federal grand jury returned an indictment on March 5, 1985, charging Dr. James O. Bailes, D.C., (Doctor of Chiropractic) of High Point, North Carolina, with eight counts of mail fraud." The indictment charged that between January 1981 and August 1984, Bailes was engaged in a fraud scheme with Pedro de Mesones, to obtain an M.D. degree from CETEC University Medical School in the Dominican Republic without actually fulfilling all the requirements for such a degree. Bailes then used his M.D. diploma and transcripts from CETEC to gain a hospital residency position at the Baylor University Medical Center in Dallas, where he worked for almost two years. Bailes also used the CETEC document to apply for medical licenses in six states and was ultimately licensed as a medical doctor in Georgia and New Mexico. Bailes was arraigned in Dallas on March 22, 1985 (U.S. Postal Service, 1985, p. 19).

On March 5, 1985, the same Dallas Federal Grand Jury returned a similar 4-count mail fraud indictment against Kelly J. Murphrey, charging that between September 1981 and March 1984, he too was involved with de Mesones in obtaining a CETEC diploma and transcripts and a hospital residency position at the Baylor University Medical Center in Dallas, where he worked for over a year. He applied for licensure in two states, Wyoming and New Mexico (U.S. Postal Service, 1985, p. 19).

On March 7, 1985, Marion W. Russell, also of Dallas, pleaded guilty as a result of plea bargaining negotiations, to a one-count information filed by the U.S. Attorney's Office. The information charged him with mail fraud and stated that between July 1982 and October 1983, Russell was engaged in a fraud scheme with de Mesones to obtain an M.D. diploma and transcripts from CETEC. Armed with these documents, Russell applied for a medical license in the state of Montana and applied for a residency position at the Baylor University Medical Center (U.S. Postal Service, 1985, p. 19).

As it probed the nefarious activities of de Mesones and

The U.S. Postal Inspection Service gets its evidence of using the mails to defraud in this telephoto shot of a postman delivering express package to Pedro de Mesones's wife, Sharon, on September 13, 1982. (Courtesy of U.S. Postal Inspection Service.)

others, the Pepper Subcommittee thoroughly explored the relationship of the problem of fraudulent credentials to functions of state licensure of health care and other professionals (U.S. Congress, House, 11 December 1985, pp. 166–172).

The Question of Licensure

The Subcommittee found that the principal responsibility for receiving and acting on complaints relating to fraudulent occupational credentials rests with state licensing agencies. State efforts in this regard are confined primarily to the regulation of some occupations and degree granting institutions of higher learning. Most state officials recognize the problem of fraudulent credentials as serious and on the rise. Nevertheless, state efforts to combat such fraud are severely limited by the absence of a meaningful national information system through which states can be kept updated on pending or com-

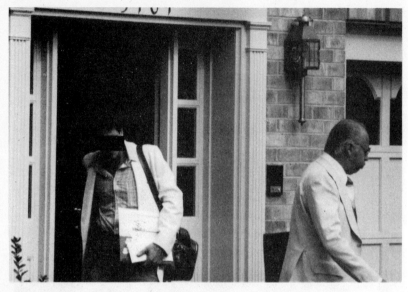

More evidence is gathered at de Mesones's Alexandria, Virginia, residence on Sep-
tember 14, 1982, when de Mesones (right) and courier (not charged) leave en route
to the airport. (Courtesy of U.S. Postal Inspection Service.)

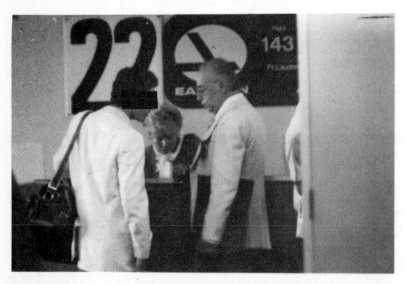

Pedro de Mesones (right) and courier under Postal Inspection Service surveillance
at Washington's National Airport. (Courtesy of U.S. Postal Inspection Service.)

Postal Inspectors (left to right) Denise Cann, David Cyr, and Randy Willetts execute search warrants in Pedro de Mesones's office. (Courtesy of U.S. Postal Inspection Service.)

pleted disciplinary actions against fraudulent practitioners. Also, current "reciprocity arrangements" between states are problematic. In some instances, this provided the opportunity for suspected or known phony practitioners to relocate their phony practices without detection by the state in which they relocated.

State regulation of professionals usually takes the form of "licensure" and some type of periodic review. "Licensure," as defined by the U.S. Department of Health and Human Services, is "the process by which a government agency grants permission to an individual to engage in a given occupation upon finding that the applicant has attained the minimal degree of competency necessary to ensure that the public health, safety, and welfare will be reasonably protected." Since state law establishing a licensed occupation usually sets forth the "scope of practice" covered by the act, licensing laws are often

It's written in Spanish but it's as good as gold. U.S. Postal Inspection Service operative Odette Bouchard acquired this diploma certifying her as a "Doctor of Medicine" from CETEC University in the Dominican Republic. (Courtesy of U.S. Postal Inspection Service.)

also referred to as "practice acts" (U.S. Congress, House, 11 December 1985, p. 166).

Before a license for an occupation or profession is granted, the applicant is supposed to meet certain requirements as set forth in state law. These usually include training and experience, minimum age, years of formal education or academic degree and a period of residence within the state. Most of the licensed professions are monitored by licensure boards who review applications to determine whether or not the applicant meets the standards set for that particular profession by the state. Licensure boards also are responsible for reviewing complaints against license holders and disciplining license

UNIVERSIDAD CETEC
Founded July 19, 1971
Santo Domingo, Dominican Republic

ACADEMIC RECORD

DATE OF BIRTH	STUDENT NUMBER	SEX	ADMITTED TO:		
APRIL 26, 1950	02-01-0685	F	SCHOOL OF MEDICINE		
STUDENT NAME			DEGREE CONFERRED:		DATE CONFERRED:
ODETTE LUCILLE BOUCHARD			DOCTOR OF MEDICINE		DEC 18, 1982

COURSE No.	DESCRIPTIVE TITLE	Cred.	Grade		COURSE No.	DESCRIPTIVE TITLE	Cred.	Grade	
	FIRST SEMESTER					**SECOND SEMESTER**			
521	HUMAN ANATOMY	10	B	APR	527	NEURO-ANATOMY	5	B	APR
524	HISTOLOGY	4	B	APR	531	BIOCHEMISTRY	8	B	APR
525	EMBRYOLOGY	2	D	APR	582	COMMUNITY HEALTH II	3	B	APR
529	GENETICS	3	B	APR	591	HUMAN BEHAVIOR I	4	B	APR
581	COMMUNITY HEALTH I	4	B	APR					
	THIRD SEMESTER					**FOURTH SEMESTER**			
541	MICROBIOLOGY	6	B	APR	561	PHARMACOLOGY	6	B	APR
542	PARASITOLOGY	2	B	APR	571	PATHOLOGY	6	B	APR
551	PHYSIOLOGY	8	D	APR	584	COMMUNITY HEALTH IV (E)	3	A	APR
583	COMMUNITY HEALTH III	3	B	APR	594	HUMAN BEHAVIOR III	4	A	APR
593	HUMAN BEHAVIOR II	4	B	APR					
	FIFTH SEMESTER					**SIXTH SEMESTER**			
572	PHYSIOPATHOLOGY	6	A	APR	631	SURGERY	14	B	APR
601	INTERNAL MEDICINE	10	B	APR					
	SEVENTH SEMESTER					**EIGHTH SEMESTER**			
611	PEDIATRICS	10	B	APR	641	FAMILY MEDICINE	10	B	APR
621	OBSTETRICS & GYNECOLOGY	10	B	APR	651	ELECTIVES	10	A	APR

SYSTEM OF STUDENT EVALUATION:

Grade	Value	Student Performance
A	4.0	Superior (90% or above)
B	3.0	Good (80% – 89%)
C	2.0	Average (75% – 79%)
D	1.0	Subaverage (70% – 74%)
F	0.0	Failure (69% or below)
I	- -	Incomplete course work
W	- -	Withdrawal by permission
APR	- -	Approved
CONV	- -	Convalidated

RECORD CERTIFIED BY:

Margarita... REGISTRAR

DEAN

12/20/82
DATE

SEAL

Postal Inspection Service operative Odette Bouchard's grades in medical school at CETEC University weren't bad according to this transcript—a notable achievement in that she never attended a class and did no work to earn her medical degree (Courtesy of U.S. Postal Inspection Service.)

holders who do not meet required state standards of performance.

There is tremendous variation between the states in what occupations are licensed, what licensure requirements are, and how stringently the requirements are enforced. In an effort to determine the range of variation in these areas, Chairman Pepper of the Subcommittee on Health and Long-Term Care sent a questionnaire in May 1985 to the Governors of all fifty states, the District of Columbia, Guam, and the Virgin Islands. The survey contained a series of questions related to the occupations licensed and the requirements for each, the identification of fraudulent credential holders, and the sharing of information among the states relative to identified cases of fraudulent credentials.

As summarized in the Subcommittee's December 11, 1985, "Hearing Record," responses from the forty-one states responding to the Subcommittee survey revealed that more than 700 occupations are regulated by one or more of the states. From barbers to doctors, from electricians to soil checkers, nearly every imaginable occupation is licensed by at least one state. Yet, there are only twenty occupations licensed by all states. They are: accountant, architect, attorney, barber, chiropractor, cosmetologist, dental hygienist, dentist, insurance agent, licensed practical nurse, optometrist, osteopath, pharmacist, physical therapist, physician/ surgeon, podiatrist, primary school teacher, real estate agent, registered nurse, and secondary school teacher (U.S. Congress, House, 11 December 1985, p. 166).

The Subcommittee was surprised to note the many glaring disparities between states in the occupations they license and those they do not. All states do license barbers and cosmetologists, yet not all license psychologists and physician assistants. All states license real estate agents, but only thirteen license elevator inspectors. Arkansas requires bug exterminators and sanitarians to be licensed to practice, yet does not have the same requirements for opticians and electricians. Kentucky licenses watchmakers and auctioneers, but does not require licenses for psychologists, building contractors, or school bus drivers. Maine licenses tree surgeons, soil testers, and movie projectionists while not requiring the same of ambulance attendants or occupational therapists. This list of apparently nonsensical disparities is hard to explain, but it is real.

The Chairman's survey of states also confirmed other information examined by the Subcommittee as to the national scope of the fraudulent credential problem in 1985. Governor after governor and state licensure board after state licensure board reported grievous cases of phony credentials they had discovered. The following represent a sample of the states' responses (U.S. Congress, House, 11 December 1985, pp. 167–168).

• South Dakota identified a case involving fraudulent engineering credentials from a resident applying for licensure with the state. He submitted fraudulent documents to the State Board including an engineering degree obtained from a diploma mill, references, and registration documents verifying his passage of national engineering exams. He was seeking a job as an electrical engineer at Ellsworth Air Force Base in South Dakota.

• Michigan reported the case of Norman W. Blevins who presented the state medical licensing board a letter from the Educational Commission of Foreign Medical Graduates. Blevins was granted a limited license based on this letter. However, it was later found that the letter had been falsified and in fact Blevins had failed the foreign medical school equivalency test three times. In the meantime, the hospital at which Blevins was practicing had suspended him on the basis of poor clinical performance. The county prosecutor's office in the Michigan township then issued a warrant against Blevins for practicing medicine without license. Blevins, however, immediately skipped to Arizona.

• Wisconsin told the Subcommittee of an engineer and a psychologist who had been licensed by the state based on falsified transcripts. The state also reported the case of a phony architect who was licensed based on his presentation of a degree in architecture. It was later revealed that his degree was fraudulent. In addition, Wisconsin told the Subcommittee that it had recently identified a woman who was falsely representing herself as a registered nurse, when in fact, she had no such credentials.

• Massachusetts identified a case involving a licensed practical nurse who had been registered by the Massachusetts Board of Registration of Nursing. The state discovered that the licensee had falsified her application representing herself as a high school graduate. The woman in question had used an alias, which was the name of a deceased person, in order to obtain a high school transcript.

A December 1984 survey by the Subcommittee on Health and Long-Term Care of State Medical Licensing Boards regarding the problem of fraudulent medical credentials also indicates the complexity and seriousness of this problem. The vast majority of boards reported receiving complaints relating to the validity or authenticity of physicians' credentials in their state. All but two responding state boards considered the problem of phony doctors a serious one.

Controlling the Fraud

Chairman Pepper's May 1985 survey of the states shed light on several problems facing the states in their efforts to control fraudulent credentials. The most serious obstacle to effective state enforcement, the Subcommittee found, involved the degree to which information on actions taken in regard to fraudulent credentials is shared between states. There is currently no national information collected and made available to all states. Instead, individual states collect bits and pieces of information on disciplinary actions taken against licensed persons and for the most part keep it to themselves.

Sharing Information. The states were asked if they routinely share information about fraudulent professionals with other states. While over half of the states reported sharing information with others, almost a third of these states only share information when it is requested by another state. In addition the states indicated that only disciplinary actions are reported and shared with other states. Thus, for example, if it is determined that an individual has either attempted to or did obtain a license by using fraudulent credentials but that disciplinary action was not initiated because the individual voluntarily left the state or quit the profession, information about the fraud may not be kept or made available to other state licensing organizations.

Those states sharing information do so primarily through the national boards representing the various state occupational licensing agencies such as the National Board of Nursing Home Administrator Examiners. Some states share information directly with other state boards through newsletters and phone calls. In 1980, the Council of State Governments formed the National Clearinghouse on Licensure, Enforcement, and Regulation (CLEAR) to strengthen the enforcement procedures and systems of state licensing authorities. In response to the problem of movement of phony and incompetent professionals from state to state, CLEAR set up the National Disciplinary Information System (NDIS). NDIS puts out a monthly listing of all disciplinary actions taken against licensed professionals in the twenty-seven states which currently participate in it. This monthly publication is the most comprehensive up-to-date national information available.

While NDIS is a step in the right direction, it clearly does not go far enough. What is really needed is a fully automated nationwide tracking system used regularly by all the states which would have current information including pending and closed disciplinary actions, recent complaints investigated by state boards, and persons identified by state boards as possessing fraudulent credentials, whether licensed or not. This information should be updated on a regular basis by the state licensing boards as well as from information referrals from other state entities (such as consumer affairs departments) and federal agencies (such as the U.S. Postal Inspection Service and the FBI) based on complaints they receive and investigations they undertake. State boards would then have fingertip access to a fairly comprehensive list of phonies across the nation.

Reciprocity in Professional Licensure. The other related hindrance to state efforts at controlling fraudulent practices

identified in the Subcommittee survey is the common arrangement between states known as "reciprocity". Reciprocity
agreements between states normally allow professionals licensed in one of the states to practice in the other without
question. Based on reciprocity agreements, the accepting state
may waive the examination or credential verification process
based on action previously taken by another state. In these
instances, the accepting state could falsely assume that an
individual's credentials or other qualifications were properly
examined at the time of initial licensing. Once fully operational, a nationwide tracking system as described would substantially reduce this problem.

Other State Controls.   A number of improvements have been
made by some states in ferreting out fraudulent credentials
though strengthening their licensing functions. Since the Subcommittee on Health and Long-Term Care's December 1984
hearing on fraudulent medical credentials, many state medical
licensing boards have taken steps to beef up their review of
medical credentials. Many have set up special subcommittees
and task forces to examine the problem of bogus credentials
and many others have installed much stricter review criteria
for graduates of foreign medical schools, while also doing a
better job of exchanging information.

Controls designed to prevent cheating on medical licensing tests are also in place in some states. These controls
include seating students in individual rooms and monitoring
by hidden video cameras. Also, the national test taken by
graduates of foreign medical schools seeking to practice in the
United States, given by the Educational Commission for Foreign Medical School Graduates, has been revamped in an effort to ensure that competency is adequately evaluated and
measured.

Some states, such as Florida, have recently instituted
stricter screening and review measures to protect residents
from fraudulent practitioners, according to the Subcommittee's December 1985 "Hearing Record." Florida now requires
applicants for teaching certificates to be fingerprinted; that
requirement should enable officials to screen out more effec-

tively those applicants who lie about their backgrounds. Since the measure went into effect, Florida officials have uncovered 225 applicants who failed to report prior arrests and convictions. About a dozen of those involved felony convictions or multiple arrest records (U.S. Congress, House, 11 December 1985, pp. 170–172).

The other major tool cited by the Subcommittee as available to the states in controlling fraudulent credentials is that of regulation of institutions offering undergraduate, graduate, and professional degrees within their boundaries. Because of the great variance in requirements relating to authorization of institutions of higher education "and because of the critical importance of assuring a minimum level of academic quality in all such entities," it was recommended that a set of suggested state standards be devised and proposed to the states. At a minimum, all states, the Subcommittee said, should require all private institutions to be licensed based on a review of their educational standards and some ongoing review to ensure continued compliance (U.S. Congress, House, 11 December 1985, p. 172).

Fraud and Federal Employees

Following up work initiated at its 1984 and 1985 hearings, the Pepper Subcommittee issued a report in April 1986 on "Fraudulent Credentials: Federal Employees." What the report and concurrent hearing suggest is that if the federal government is charged with nabbing magna cum frauds, it cannot be smug about any absence of culpability in its own household.

As part of its initial Dipscam sweep, the FBI turned up the names of some 200 federal and 200 state government employees who have purchased fraudulent degrees. A number of these individuals worked in highly sensitive positions. Examples follow.

- An engineer at Kennedy Space Center who obtained a B.S. degree in electrical engineering
- An employee with Westinghouse Nuclear International

(which contracts with the Federal government to con-
struct nuclear power plants) who acquired a B.A., M.A.,
and Ph.D. in civil engineering
- An employee with Post-Launch Operations, Kennedy Space
Center, who obtained a B.S. in mechanical engineering
- An employee with the Joint Chiefs of Staff, U.S. Army,
Pentagon, who acquired a Ph.D. in history
- An employee with the Three Mile Island Nuclear Power
Plant who obtained a B.S. in mechanical engineering
- An employee with NASA's Lyndon Johnson Space Center
in Houston, who got a Ph.D. in electrical aerospace en-
gineering
- An air traffic controller with U.S. Department of Trans-
portation Federal Aviation Center who obtained a B.A.
in aviation
- A chief deputy U.S. Marshall in California who acquired
B.S. and B.A. degrees (U.S. Congress, House, April 1986,
p. 7).

The Subcommittee's hearing record concludes with responses
received from federal agency officials charged with investigating the findings with respect to questionable degrees held
by some of their employees. Letters from some of the degree
holders are also included. The usual response of these employees is either that they believed themselves to be receiving
legitimate degrees or that they may have acquired spurious
degrees but never used them to secure employment, promotion, or other advantage (U.S. Congress, House, 18 April
1986, pp. 9–71).

As is amply demonstrated by the work of the two subcommittees of the House Select Committee on Aging, the
problem of fraudulent occupational licensure is intertwined
with the related problem of fraudulent academic credentials.
As Representative Pepper has stated, "the American public
will continue to fall prey to 'paper' professionals unless corrective action is taken."

8
When Is a Degree Not a Degree?

When such information is provided at all, a certain lack of precision appears deliberate in the typical diploma mill description of credit and degrees. Quarter or semester credit hours are seldom defined or applied in any consistent way. Course offerings may never be defined by a syllabus or comparable document. Where syllabi do exist or must be generated because of state requirements, they may be copied or adapted with few alterations from syllabi used at legitimate higher education institutions. The major and minor areas of degree-study may not be delineated, and narrowly professional degrees, for example, nutrition, may be designated on diplomas stemming from a curriculum suggesting a much more general program such as health sciences.

To find a roadmap through the maze of diploma mill credentials, it is helpful to clarify the common base of assumptions within the higher education community about the term

"credit" and the designations of degrees (associate, baccalaureate, master's, and doctoral).

Among the academic terms most abused by diploma mills
is that of educational credit. Credit for "life experience" is
awarded by these institutions in the same cavalier manner as
credit for completion of their pseudo-correspondence courses.
Quality academic institutions award credit for demonstrated
learning, not experience.

Historically, credit has been and continues to be essentially a method of recording time spent in a classroom and/or
laboratory in learning postsecondary-level knowledge or skills.
As the complexity of the learning experience increases so does
the length of time required and the amount and/or level of
credit assigned to it. In recent years, credit has also been
used to quantify and record the outcomes of learning acquired
outside the sponsorship of legally authorized and accredited
institutions. In the most contemporary context, then, credit
is defined in terms of time, but is intended as a measure of
the extent and profundity of learning outcomes.

It is the responsibility of a postsecondary institution's
faculty to evaluate learning outcomes and to determine the
amount and level of credit assigned them regardless of the
manner in which such learning is acquired. When learning
presented for credit evaluation emanates from outside an institution, the outcomes need to be evaluated by duly appointed
faculty and should be judged equivalent to learning acquired
through classroom and laboratory learning experiences. Campus-based faculty who have intimate knowledge of an institution's degree programs have a base of resources and experience from which to make informed judgments. A diploma
mill, on the other hand, has no proper base of academic resources. Reviews, if any, which it conducts of extrainstitutional learning are neither systematic nor criterion-oriented.

Semester credit hours and *quarter credit hours* are the
two most commonly used systems for measuring and recording course work and/or learning outcomes. Definitions of credit
hours are not rigid, but these guideline statements would be
considered acceptable at most respectable American colleges
and universities.

Semester credit hours are based on the semester calendar which usually extends for about fifteen weeks. One semester credit hour normally signifies fifteen hours of classroom contact plus at least thirty hours of outside preparation or the equivalent. For laboratory work, one semester credit hour normally signifies thirty hours of laboratory, plus necessary outside preparation or the equivalent. One semester credit hour may also signify not less than forty-five hours of shop instruction or the equivalent.

Quarter credit hours are based on the quarter calendar which usually extends for about ten weeks. The usual custom is to equate two semester hours with three quarter hours.

It would be more comfortable to chastise diploma mills for their casual or nonexistent definitions of degrees if there were a higher degree of consensus among legitimate institutions about what a degree really is. The higher education community is vulnerable to attack from the diploma mill crowd on this score. A number of attempts at degree definition have been made. Some have received a fair amount of praise, but the academic landscape is strewn with the wreckage of many failed endeavors.

But if academic definitions of the various postsecondary education degrees are less than standardized, there is nonetheless a wide body of assumptions bearing on degree integrity that are shared by the higher education community. The terms associate degree, baccalaureate degree, master's degree, and doctoral degree have meaning in this sense.

The Associate Degree

Associate degrees are central to the academic mission at most community, technical, and junior colleges. On that account, it is not surprising that the most definitive statements about the associate degree to date have been produced by the American Association of Community and Junior Colleges (AACJC). However, an excellent statement entitled "Associate Degree Standards" was also developed by the Minnesota Higher Education Coordinating Board in 1986.

In its "Policy Statement on the Associate Degree" issued

in July 1984, AACJC affirms that the associate degree "should consist of a coherent and tightly knit sequence of courses that includes a general education core capped by an evaluation process that measures the outcomes of the learning process, either at the course level, comprehensively, or both." All such programs "must include the opportunity for the student to demonstrate proficiency in the use of language and computation, for whatever their career goals, students will be called upon to exercise competence in these areas."

In addition, AACJC asserts that all associate degree programs

> must reflect those characteristics that help define what constitutes an educated person. Such characteristics include a level of general education that enables the individual to understand and appreciate his/her culture and environment; the development of a system of personal values based on accepted ethics that lead to civic and social responsibility; and the attainment of skills in analysis, communication, quantification, and synthesis necessary for further growth as a lifespan learner and a productive member of society.

While it is understood that not all of these elements are necessarily attained through organized courses, the sponsoring institution has a responsibility to provide an intellectual and social climate that is conducive to such learning. It is also an institutional responsibility to develop appropriate procedures for assessing required learning gained outside the formal course structure.

The associate degree should be designed to be an indication that a student has attained the knowledge and skills necessary to enter a field of work or an upper division, that is, the junior and senior years of a college program. The associate degree program in arts or in science is designed primarily to prepare students to transfer to an upper-division baccalaureate degree program, and the associate in applied science degree is designed to lead the individual directly to employment in a specific career or occupation.

In April of 1986, AACJC carried its definition of the associate degree a step further as it approved a policy statement concerning the Associate in Applied Science Degree. This common variant of the associate degree is designed primarily to prepare students for immediate employment in a career field without foregoing the opportunity for further education. Among fourteen "criteria for excellence" in the Associate of Applied Science Degree, AACJC includes a number that are invariably absent in ersatz degree programs. Among these are provision for:

1. Assessment of the adequacy of each course in meeting stated outcomes
2. The minimum in degree programs of 25 percent of course credits being in general education, and a combination of general education and related studies contributing up to 50 percent of course credits
3. Student support services designed systematically for the needs of career-oriented adults
4. Degree curricula articulated with appropriate general and vocational secondary schools.

In its statement, the Minnesota Higher Education Coordinating Board notes that associate degrees are designed to accomplish one of two objectives: to help a student prepare for an occupation, or to provide a foundation for a baccalaureate degree program. Like AACJC, the Minnesota Board also emphasizes that associate degrees should be awarded for completion of a "coherent and organized set of experiences." Nonchalant and unsystematic acquisition of course credits is not enough to enable a student to qualify for the degree recognition that an associate degree can afford.

Two academic years of study are typically required for a *full-time* student to acquire the associate degree. Credit hour requirements for the associate degree typically range from 60 to 72 semester credit hours or 90 to 108 quarter credit hours. Credit should not be awarded for remedial or developmental work designed to prepare students to enter postsecondary level educational programs.

The Bachelor's Degree

Just what does it mean if one holds a baccalaureate or bachelor's degree? The academic community isn't quite sure. Much of the controversy involves questions regarding the emphasis that should be given in a curriculum to career or technical education in relation to education in the liberal arts and sciences. No clear consensus has yet emerged.

In February 1985, the Association of American Colleges (AAC), issued a report by a select committee chaired by Mark H. Curtis, entitled "Integrity in the College Curriculum: A Report to the Academic Community." The Committee, perhaps understandably, ducked the task of developing a straight-out definition of the baccalaureate degree. It did, however, come up with a "minimum required program of study for all students" in baccalaureate programs, one consisting of "intellectual, aesthetic, and philosophic experiences that should enter into the lives of men and women engaged in baccalaureate education."

The committee carefully and explicitly declined to specify "a set of required subjects or academic disciplines" as essential in a soundly conceived baccalaureate degree program. Instead, it stated nine "experiences," all of them considered as "basic to a coherent undergraduate education." These experiences are:

1. Inquiry, abstract logical thinking, critical analysis
2. Literacy including writing, reading, speaking, listening
3. Understanding numerical data
4. Historical consciousness
5. Science
6. Values
7. Art
8. International and multicultural experiences
9. Study in depth.

The AAC select committee, in concluding its report, noted that the academic community and the general public are "uneasy with the evidence of the decline and devaluation of the bachelor's degree in the recent past." It called for "a renewal of the faculty's corporate responsibility for the curriculum." It cited its "nine basic intellectual, aesthetic, and philosophic experiences as a design for diverting the course of study from chaos."

Study toward a baccalaureate degree (in the absence of awards of credit for college-level extra-institutional learning) typically requires about four years and a minimum of 120 semester or 180 quarter units of study by a *full-time* student. Baccalaureate degrees in professional fields usually require more than these minimums.

The Master's Degree

In April 1981, the Council of Graduate Schools in the United States (CGS) published a policy statement in which it defined the master's degree as "customarily awarded to an aspirant who achieves a level of academic accomplishment substantially beyond that required for the Baccalaureate degree." Such a degree program "should consist of a coherent pattern of courses frequently capped by comprehensive examinations and a thesis or its equivalent in a creative project." The CGS statement notes that ideally a master's degree program "should include an opportunity for the student to learn to present information in written and oral form to a variety of audiences."

There are two basic types of master's degree programs: (1) academic degrees, the master of arts (M.A.) or the master of science (M.S.); and (2) professional degrees which are awarded for academic accomplishment in professional fields and often serve as preparation for careers in the various professions. The names used to designate the professional degree are often stated as "Master of ____ [Professional Degree]."

A separate administrative entity within a university is ordinarily required if even a few master's degrees are to be developed and administered effectively, according to the CGS report. A graduate faculty, academically responsible for all graduate programs, is responsible to a graduate dean. If he or she is to be effective as the principal academic officer, the graduate dean "should be a recognized scholar or expert in a specific field, have experience in graduate education, and be accepted as a peer by the graduate faculty."

The Doctoral Degree

An occasional paper entitled "The American Doctorate in the Context of New Patterns in Higher Education" by John

W. Harris, William E. Troutt, and Grover J. Andrews, was released by the Council on Postsecondary Accreditation (COPA) in 1980. With an introduction by Michael J. Pelczar, Jr., then President of the Council of Graduate Schools (CGS) in the United States, this paper does much to clarify the meaning of the American doctorate at a time when its integrity is threatened.

The authors of the COPA paper cite the following "broad achievements" as the foundation blocks for the American doctorate: (1) a demonstrable mastery of a distinct, recognized field of graduate study; (2) possession of a pertinent research or scholarship skill; and (3) design and completion of a significant work of scholarship or research in one's designated field of mastery.

CGS describes the typical doctoral program as consisting of:

> lectures, seminars, discussions, independent study, and research designed to help the students make significant contributions to knowledge in a reasonable time. During the first year or two of study, doctoral students usually take formal courses and seminars and may begin research shortly after entering the program, although, initially, most of the effort will be devoted to acquiring a working knowledge of the field through study of the literature. In many institutions, after the formal course work has been largely completed, the language and/or other research tool proficiency examinations have been passed, and the comprehensive (qualifying or preliminary) written and oral examinations have been successfully completed, the students are "admitted to candidacy" for the doctoral degree (Council of Graduate Schools, 1982, p. 7).

The doctoral student devotes essentially full time to completing the dissertation research planned with the adviser, or major professor, and the graduate committee. An oral defense of the research and dissertation by the candidate before the graduate committee and other persons invited to attend constitutes the final examination.

The Ph.D. dissertation fulfills two major purposes. On one level, a dissertation is an intensive, highly professional educational experience, the successful completion of which demonstrates that the candidate can carry out and communicate on scholarly research at a high level of professional competence. On another level, its results constitute a contribution to knowledge in the field.

Not every doctorate is a Ph.D. Professional doctorates (the originals were in the fields of law, medicine, and theology), unlike the Ph.D., are not research degrees. They instead represent a *practitioner's* degree and tend to be awarded after completion of a rigorous standardized curriculum, often guided by professional association recommendations and shaped by state licensing agencies (Harris, Troutt, and Andrews, 1980, p. 10). These programs usually require an essay that deals in depth with a topic relating to the professional field or major area of study.

Because it is so demanding in its legitimate forms, study toward the doctoral degree is often uncompleted or aspirants settle for the master's degree or something less. A study by Ellen Benkin of students beginning work toward the doctoral degree at the University of California–Los Angeles in the years between 1969 and 1971 reveals a pattern that is probably typical. She found that by 1982, 31 percent of the original number of students had not acquired the doctoral or any other advanced degree; 40 percent had acquired master's degrees; 6 percent had completed all requirements except the dissertation for the doctoral degree; and only 24 percent had reached their original goal of earning the doctoral degree (Benkin, 1987).

Students enrolled in doctoral programs on a *full-time* basis can usually finish within four or five years after receiving the baccalaureate degree. However, since many graduate students enroll on a part-time basis, the time required for them to complete all requirements is longer. In 1983, the median number of years required for a student to move from a baccalaureate degree to a doctorate (all fields) was 6.8, according to ACE's *1986–87 Fact Book on Higher Education*.

How might the quality of information conveyed on educational credit and credentials be maintained and approved? In 1978, the Board of Directors of ACE approved a statement entitled "Recommendations on Credentialing Educational Accomplishment," that had been developed by a task force on educational credit and credentials of the organization's Commission on Educational Credit.

In the ACE statement, confidence in the American system of credit and credentials for postsecondary education was reaffirmed—though it was noted that the system should be modified so that it more adequately serves present-day educational and social needs. The "primary responsibility" for awarding degrees, it was asserted, "should remain with the faculties, administrators, and boards of control of accredited institutions that are legally authorized to grant such formal recognition." Institutions or organizations lacking the proper degree-granting structure were to limit their awards to certificates or other credentials whose designations are clearly distinguishable from degrees. Furthermore, undergraduate degrees were not to be awarded by any institution for programs lacking a general/liberal education component.

The ACE policy makers specified that associate and baccalaureate degrees should attest to at least three types of accomplishment: (1) accomplishment specified by the awarding institution as necessary for the development of a broadly educated person, including familiarity with general areas of knowledge; (2) competence in analytical, communication, quantitative, and synthesizing skills; and (3) accomplishment in a specialized area of study covering a set of integrated learnings requiring analysis, understanding of principles that have judgmental application, and a theoretical knowledge base.

In the statement, ACE went on record in favor of sound and well-designed programs of nontraditional education—a fact that punctures diploma mill charges that nontraditional approaches are not permitted under educational philosophy prevailing at traditional academic institutions. "Alternative programs" at the postsecondary education level were to state requirements in terms of assessable educational accomplishment and to permit students to demonstrate accomplishment without reference to time-bound and campus-bound instruction and learning. "High priority" was to be given to developing improved and technically sound approaches for evaluating educational accomplishment and for assessing equivalent learning attained in extrainstitutional settings.

Credit was to be awarded for educational accomplishment attained in extrainstitutional settings. The needs of "mobile and older adult students" should be considered. These students should be provided with "sufficient information, orientation, and counseling on the requirements for credentials and on the policies for the transfer of credit and for the award of credit for extrainstitutional learning."

The concept of residence study was to be examined to assure that such requirements had "educational validity." Interinstitutional efforts aimed at developing articulation agreements relating to transfer policies should be encouraged, the objective being to eliminate "arbitrary agreements" and "arbitrary transfer barriers."

All of these affirmations were designed to encourage traditional education institutions to adapt their programs and support services to serve better the needs of mature adult students. Unfortunately, academic faculties have been slow in responding to these challenges.

In summary, degree definitions in the United States—especially for the baccalaureate—are in a state of flux. College and university faculties are wrestling with difficult questions as they seek sound and acceptable redefinitions in keeping with the times, and occasionally, this debate results in uncertainty and confusion within the academic community. With their careless or misleading use of degree definitions, diploma mills have been quick to capitalize on this ambiguity.

9

The Uses and Abuses
of Accreditation

There are four basic facts that the layman ought to know about accreditation. First, it is a uniquely American institution. Second, accreditation comes in two varieties, institutional (sometimes called "regional" or "national"), and specialized. Third, accrediting bodies are themselves "accredited." And, lastly, much diploma mill fraud is perpetuated by misleading information about accreditation. An examination of each of these statements will provide some insight into accreditation as a safeguard against diploma mill operations. It will be seen also that inadequate accreditation or pseudo-accreditation can be a formidable weapon in the hands of unscrupulous diploma mill operators.

In their excellent book, *Understanding Accreditation*, Kenneth E. Young, et al. cite this definition of the process of accreditation:

Postsecondary accreditation is a process by which an institution or a specialized unit of postsecondary education periodically evaluates its educational activities and seeks an independent judgment by peers that it achieves substantially its own educational objectives and meets the established standards of the body by which it seeks accreditation. Generally the accreditation process involves (1) a clear statement of the institution's or unit's educational objectives; (2) a self-study by the institution or unit which examines its activities in relation to those objectives; (3) an on-site evaluation by a selected group of peers which reports to the accrediting body; and (4) a decision by this independent body that the institution or unit does or does not meet its standards for accreditation. (Young et al., p. 449).

Much of the following information about accreditation is taken from a "Policy Statement on the Role and Value of Accreditation" that was adopted by the Board of the Council on Postsecondary Accreditation (COPA) in 1982. As such, it may be considered as a widely accepted view of accreditation as it is currently understood and applied at most American colleges and universities.

What is accreditation? Accreditation has two fundamental purposes: to assure the quality of the institution or program and to assist in the improvement of the institution or program.

In most countries of the world, the government, through its Ministry of Education, supervises and controls educational institutions. The federal government in the United States has never had a comparable role. The U.S. Department of Education does not authorize, approve, or accredit postsecondary education institutions. However, the Department does publish a list of nationally recognized accrediting agencies which it determines to be "reliable authorities" as to the quality of training offered by educational institutions and programs. (See description in chapter 12.) The system of voluntary accreditation involves review of an institution's academic and other programs by nongovernmental bodies.

The groups conducting institutional accreditation are national or regional in scope and comprise the institutions that have achieved and maintain accreditation. A specialized body conducting accreditation of a program preparing students for a profession or occupation is national in scope and is often closely associated with professional associations in the field.

Institutional or specialized accreditation cannot, of course, guarantee the quality of individual graduates of a program or of individual courses within an institution or program, but it does give reasonable assurance of the context and quality of the education offered.

In the United States to speak of an institution as accredited usually means accreditation by an agency recognized by COPA. This body requires its members (institutional and specialized accrediting agencies) to meet criteria with respect to standards, procedures, and organization regarded as necessary for the effective conduct of the accrediting process. A COPA-recognized accrediting body can be regarded as qualified to conduct evaluations of institutions and/or programs seeking accreditation, and accreditation by such COPA-approved bodies is generally recognized and accepted in higher education.

Both institutional and specialized accrediting bodies conduct the accreditation process using a common pattern. The pattern requires that three criteria be met. One, a rigorous and candid self-study by the institution or program must examine and evaluate its mission, objectives, activities, and achievements. Two, an on-site visit by a team of peers must occur. This team makes judgments on the degree to which an institution or program is fulfilling its mission and meeting its objectives; they provide expert criticism and offer suggestions for improvement. Three, a subsequent review and decision must be made by a central governing commission or board. Within this general pattern the various accrediting bodies have developed a variety of individual procedures adapted to their own circumstances. Over the past few years, increasing attention has been given to the achievement of educational outcomes by students as a basis for making judgments about the effectiveness and quality of institutions and programs.

With respect to academic degrees, *institutional* accreditation is designed to assure that the institution:

1. Has appropriate purposes
2. Has the resources needed to accomplish its purposes
3. Can demonstrate that it is accomplishing its purposes
4. Gives reason to believe that it will continue to accomplish its purposes.

Institutional accrediting bodies consider the characteristics of institutions as a whole. For this reason not only the educational program of the institutions is evaluated, but also other institutional characteristics such as adequacy of library and learning resources, student personnel services, financial conditions, effective management, student assessment, short- and long-range planning, and administrative strength. Educational programs are reviewed as a part of consideration of the entire institution, but not in great detail.

The criteria of an institutional accrediting body are broad, as is demanded by the attention to the whole institution and by the number of postsecondary institutions of widely different purposes and scopes. Such criteria also provide encouragement to institutions to develop and try innovative curricula and procedures and to adopt them when they prove successful. The institutions are judged primarily in terms of their mission and objectives as stated by themselves, not by the evaluating accrediting body.

What does it mean to say that an institution has been awarded accredited status? In a 1986 speech (since published by the College Board) William J. MacLeod provided a seasoned answer.* "It means that the characteristics of the total institution have been considered and that the total pattern of institutional strengths and weakness has been weighed." The institution has been found to have "educationally appropriate objectives" for carrying out its mission, as well as the resources necessary to achieve these objectives. It further means that the institution has demonstrated that it is in fact achieving these objectives at the time of accreditation and has provided sufficient evidence to support the belief that it will continue to achieve its objectives over a reasonable future.

*Reprinted with permission from *Overseas Educational Advisors' Manual*, copyright © 1987 by College Entrance Examination Board, New York.

"Institutional accreditation," MacLeod notes, "therefore *does not mean* that all aspects of institutional life have been found to be of equal quality, but that, as a whole, the institution is doing the job it claims to be doing. It does not mean that all of its educational programs are on the same level of quality, but that no part has been found to be so weak that the overall educational effectiveness of the institution and its services to students is being undermined." Since *institutional* accreditation does not imply specific accreditation of any particular program in the institution, diploma mill claims such as "this program is accredited" or "this degree is accredited" are incorrect and misleading.

While the granting of accreditation indicates "an acceptable level of institutional quality," according to MacLeod, "any institution, however excellent, is capable of improvement, which must come from its own clear identification and understanding of its strengths and weaknesses. Institutional improvement is encouraged by the requirement that the accredited institution must conduct periodic self-evaluations seeking to identify what the institution does well, determining the areas in which improvement is needed, and developing plans to address needed improvements. Such re-evaluations must take place at least every ten years, but annual reports and a fifth-year comprehensive report are usually required by the accrediting agency. In addition, the accrediting bodies reserve the right to review member institutions for cause at any time. The institutional accrediting bodies also encourage institutional improvement through the advice and counsel provided by the visiting team, which comprises educators drawn primarily from accredited institutions, and by the publications and other services of the accrediting bodies that address various issues and problems of institutional life" (College Board, 1987).

Institutional accrediting bodies may initially grant "Candidate for Accreditation" status to institutions applying for eventual accreditation. This status is by no means automatic. Typically, a preliminary self-study followed up by a site visit is required. Candidacy for accreditation is not accreditation; neither does it assure eventual accreditation. It is simply a sign that an institution is progressing toward accreditation in a manner acceptable to the institutional accrediting agency. Institutions holding official candidacy status may, however, be afforded some of the rights and privileges enjoyed by fully accredited colleges and universities (e.g., eligibility for certain federal funds).

At present, the nation is served by six regional institutional accrediting associations, all of them members of COPA. They are: Middle States Association of Colleges and Schools, New England Association of Schools and Colleges, North Central Association of Schools and Colleges, Northwest Association of Schools and Colleges, Southern Association of Colleges and Schools and Western Association of Schools and Colleges. The addresses of these organizations and the states in which they function appear in *Accredited Institutions of Postsecondary Education* published annually by the ACE, Washington, D.C., for COPA.

In addition, there are currently five COPA-recognized *institutional* accrediting commissions or entities whose scope is national and which accredit specialized institutions. They are: American Association of Bible Colleges, Association of Independent Colleges and Schools, Association of Theological Schools in the United States and Canada, National Association of Trade and Technical Schools, and National Home Study Council.

Specialized accreditation provides assurances about the adequacy of educational programs in disciplinary, professional, and occupational fields where improper activities might cause irreparable harm to members of society. To some degree, specialized accreditation also implies certain basic similarities of curriculum and degree requirements across institutional lines.

A specialized accrediting body, according to MacLeod, focuses attention on a particular professional, occupational, or disciplinary area, (e.g., nursing, physical therapy, social work, or home economics) either within an institution of higher education or at freestanding (independent) institutions (e.g., hospitals, clinics) which offer only the particular discipline or program of study. Specialized accrediting bodies are usually

closely related both to the educational programs they accredit
and to the professional association of practitioners in those
areas. Where, as is usually the case, the programs are in
larger, more complex institutions, the specialized accrediting
bodies usually require that the institution be institutionally
accredited by a COPA-recognized agency before consideration
can be given to program accreditation. When the specialized
accrediting bodies deal with freestanding, single-purpose institutions, they are expected to base their decisions on comprehensive, institution-based criteria.

Specialized accreditation usually applies to particular
professional or occupational fields in which there is a recognized first professional degree. These are areas in which public
health, welfare, safety, and/or need for assurance of professional competence are matters of academic, professional, and
public concern. With some exceptions (e.g., music, art, in-
terior design), specialized accreditation normally does not apply to the liberal arts and sciences that are considered integral
to the institutional core of educational offerings. These disciplines are considered within the purview of institutional accreditation.

*What does it mean to say that a program has been ac-
credited by a specialized accrediting body recognized by COPA?*
It means that the specific program in a given field has been
evaluated in depth according to criteria developed by educators and practicing professionals in that field and has been
found to meet or exceed those criteria. The specialized accrediting body is not unconcerned about the institution as a
whole and the educational pattern it presents. Its accreditation requirements are, however, more sharply directed to the
content of the program, including specific requirements for
resources needed to provide a program for satisfactory professional or occupational preparation. It therefore considers the
total institutional educational pattern relevant as it affects
the particular program.

Specialized accrediting bodies encourage program improvement by setting accreditation requirements as specific
goals to be achieved. In addition, assistance for program improvement is provided through the counsel of the visiting

team which includes practitioners of the profession or occupation and experienced faculty members and administrators from other institutions. Like the institutional accrediting bodies, specialized accrediting bodies require periodic formal reevaluations; the average interval between such evaluations is six to seven years.

Examples of specialized accrediting agencies are the National Architectural Accrediting Board (first professional degree programs in architecture), the Accrediting Council on Education in Journalism and Mass Communications (units and programs leading to bachelor's and master's degrees), National League for Nursing (associate, baccalaureate, and higher degree programs; also diploma and practical nurse programs), and the National Council for the Accreditation of Teacher Education (baccalaureate and graduate degree programs in teacher education). Names and addresses of specialized accrediting agencies recognized by COPA appear in *Accredited Institutions of Postsecondary Education*, which is updated and published annually (see Appendix B).

Whatever its focus, the accrediting process typically begins with an institutional or programmatic self-study, a comprehensive effort to measure progress toward previously adopted objectives. The self-study considers the interests of a broad cross-section of constituencies—students, faculty, administrators, alumni, trustees, and, in some circumstances, the local community.

The resulting report is reviewed by the appropriate accrediting commission and serves as the basis for evaluation by a site-visit team from the accrediting group. The site-visit team normally consists of professional educators (faculty and administrators), specialists selected according to the nature of the institution, and members representing specific public interests. The visiting team assesses the institution or program in light of the self-study and adds judgments based on its own expertise and its external perspective. The team prepares an evaluation report, which is reviewed by the institution or program for factual accuracy.

The original self-study, the team report, and any response the institution or program may wish to make are then forwarded to the accreditation commission. The review body uses these materials as the basis for action on the accreditation status of the institution or program. Negative actions may be appealed according to established procedures of the accrediting body.

Although accreditation is generally granted for a specific term (e.g., five or ten years), accrediting bodies reserve the right to review member institutions or programs for cause at any time. They also reserve the right to review any substantive change, such as an expansion from undergraduate to graduate offerings. Such changes may require prior approval and/or review upon implementation. In this way, accrediting bodies hold their member institutions and programs continually responsible to their educational peers, to the constituents they serve, and to the public.

The concept of accreditation, since its inception in America, represents the higher education community's principal means for quality assessment and self-regulation. In the United States the hub of this voluntary accreditation activity is COPA. COPA is a nongovernmental organization that works to foster and facilitate the role of accrediting bodies in promoting and insuring the quality and universality of American postsecondary education. COPA member accrediting bodies, while established and supported by their membership, are intended to serve the broader interest of society as well. To promote these ends, COPA sees its role as recognizing, coordinating, and periodically reviewing the work of its member accrediting bodies, and the appropriateness of existing or proposed accrediting bodies and their activities, through its granting of recognition and performance of other related functions. This portion of the COPA role is carried out largely by its Committee on Recognition.

COPA does not accredit; it grants *recognition* to those bodies which meet its criteria on standards, organizational structure, scope, public responsibility, evaluation practices and procedures, and educational philosophy and related procedures. The accrediting body must be nongovernmental and must require, as an integral part of its evaluative process, a self-analysis of the program or institution and an on-site review by a visiting team (or a validated equivalent of an on-site review). Organizations that "approve" programs without these components of the process are ineligible for COPA recognition. The recognition process is one carried on by peers and involves a review of applications by members of the Committee on Recognition and reader/consultants and a public hearing before the Committee on Recognition. The Committee's recommendations are then forwarded to the COPA Board for final action.

In the United States, an accrediting body generally has little or no clout in the higher education world unless it undergoes this review process and is accepted into COPA. This nicety, however, is conveniently ignored by the "accrediting" entity that is merely an aggregation of diploma mills or institutions not having COPA-recognized accreditation. Some diploma mills or marginal institutions can rightly claim accreditation. No argument there. But it is also true that such accreditation is virtually worthless in the real world of higher education. It still will not enable the institution to award degrees and grant credit that generally will be recognized by most American colleges and universities.

Unaccredited institutions may also claim that state governmental authorization or approval is the same as, or equivalent to, accreditation by a COPA-recognized agency. This practice, which is lamentably prevalent among *some* authorized or approved institutions in California, has caused great confusion in the minds of some customers of postsecondary education programs in that state and elsewhere. (State government regulation of postsecondary education is discussed in chapter 10, and a fuller description of California's unique laws and practices with respect to authorization, approval, and accreditation appears in chapter 11.)

Quality assurance in off-campus programming has been a source of concern to accrediting agencies. In 1980, COPA reported results of a study of off-campus postsecondary education programs on military bases (Allen and Andrews, 1980). In 1983, COPA issued a policy statement that called attention to "increasing evidence that at least a handful of colleges and universities apparently have established off-campus degree programs that are not equivalent academically to similar programs on campus, and further that they have allowed these off-campus programs to operate without adequate supervision from the sponsoring institutions." Many of these programs operate under agreements between public colleges or private universities and military installations (Council on Postsecondary Accreditation, 20 April 1983).

Off-campus or satellite programs in states or foreign countries far from the sponsoring institution present administrative and academic difficulties that are not always given careful attention. Such programs may operate without approval or review from the state or nation in which the instruction takes place. In California, for example, the Private Postsecondary Education Division is careful to state that it does not consider its review responsibilities as covering activities in states or jurisdictions other than California. This very conservative interpretation of state authority allows the vast international networks operated by some of the institutions organized under Sections 94310.2 and 94310.3, of the California Education Code to exist and expand without review by the California regulatory authorities.

Although COPA, of course, has no direct authority to regulate off-campus programs, in a statement adopted by its Board on April 20, 1983, it does specify that its member accrediting bodies are responsible for assuring the integrity of *all* programs of an institution, wherever located. Furthermore, a COPA-recognized accrediting entity is not to lend its accreditation to "unaccredited organizations or persons who operate as contractors to develop and market educational programs" (Council on Postsecondary Accreditation, 20 April 1983). Adherence to this standard is noticeably absent from procedures followed by some questionable accrediting entities. State regulatory agencies may also be deficient in regulating off-campus activities no matter how good they may be in their "immediate" jurisdiction.

The Southern Association of Colleges and Schools (SACS), the recognized institutional accrediting body in eleven southern states, specifies procedures that are typical for encouraging quality in off-campus programming. SACS requires full reports of all off-campus activities involving the granting of credit and makes it plain that all necessary approvals by state agencies must be obtained by institutions involved in decentralized programs. SACS also specifies that separate accreditation status may be required when an off-campus unit offering degree programs develops "a significant degree of autonomy and complexity."

Some diploma mills have found it expedient to claim, or imply, that they are correspondence schools or profit-making institutions and on that account are not eligible for accreditation. But they are eligible. The *for*-profit sector of American postsecondary education accrediting enterprise has three major groups, all of them COPA members. The fact that an institution offers correspondence instruction is not in itself a barrier to positive review by these bodies.

The National Home Study Council (NHSC) accredits some ninety-one institutions offering courses and programs via correspondence. Eight of these institutions offer associate degree programs; two of them offer baccalaureate degrees. Interviewed in April 1987, Michael P. Lambert, Assistant Director of NHSC, expressed some skepticism about high-speed degrees awarded by mail. He correctly describes legitimate correspondence study as "an arduous undertaking, and anybody who says it isn't is simply uninformed." Lambert indicated that "just to earn an associate's degree by correspondence study can easily take you three or four years!" (Ludlow, 1987, p. 68). A baccalaurate degree earned under the sponsorship of an NHSC-accredited institution is unlikely to be completed by even the most able and motivated student in less than four or five years.

The Accrediting Commission of the Association of Independent Colleges and Schools (AICS) accredits approximately 640 private institutions (business schools, junior and senior colleges) which offer associate, baccalaureate, and master's degrees, as well as certificates, diplomas, and special degrees. The Accrediting Commission of the National Association of Trade and Technical Schools (NATTS) accredits some 1,080 private trade and technical schools which offer courses and programs in everything from barbering to electronics. Approximately 10 percent of these award associate degrees.

While the standards and procedures specified by COPA are not, of course, fail-safe, it is extremely unlikely that an organization qualifying as a diploma mill as defined for this volume could achieve accreditation by a COPA-recognized agency. Recognizing this, some diploma mills have organized entities that purport to "accredit," "approve," or otherwise sanction their activities.

What does it take to start up an accrediting agency? Nothing except simple incorporation—which is why any analysis of the diploma mill problem must concurrently deal with the related problem of the accreditation mill.

Like its close cousin, the diploma factory, the accreditation mill is an elusive customer. Often, such entities exist only on paper or in the promotional materials of their constituent diploma mills. Standards and procedures used by these bodies, where they exist at all, are extremely questionable as safeguards for academic quality. In some instances, the spurious accrediting agency will be controlled by, and operate from the same address as, a diploma mill that it accredits.

One alleged accrediting body, for example, consists of a telephone in the living room of a residence in a large city. After 11 A.M., the resident of the apartment answers the phone with the name of the accrediting agency. An organization receives accreditation from this agency simply by paying a monthly fee. No site visits are made; normal accreditation standards, procedures, and rules are not used; and there has been what is called "open enrollment" of new members.

Another example was uncovered by the U.S. House of Representative's Select Committee on Aging, Subcommittee on Health and Long-Term Care, during its investigation of fraudulent credentials. After it set up its own diploma mill, "Capitol Institute of Advanced Education," Subcommittee staff members called a number of alleged accrediting bodies to investigate the possibility of acquiring accreditation. No one at any of the numbers called answered the telephone. Instead, answering machines presented recorded messages and asked callers to leave a message.

Within six hours, according to the Subcommittee's official hearing record, a call was received back from a Dr. George S. Reuter, Jr., President of the International Accrediting Commission of Schools, Colleges, and Theological Seminaries based in Holden, Missouri. Reuter was told by a Subcommittee staff member that a new school was being started and accreditation was needed. Reuter is quoted as saying that for a $200 fee, Capitol Institute would be instantly granted "pre-certification status" with the International Accrediting Commission. He asked no questions about the quality, degree requirements, faculty, or state authorization status of the Institute. Reuter said that full accreditation would cost an additional $660, including $50 for an official certification plaque. He further told the Subcommittee staff member that his Commission's services were comprehensive including a reference service for potential students, "registration" with the Library of Congress, and expert guidance in setting up and operating the institution (U.S. Congress, House, 11 December 1985, p. 135).

Because of its limited funds, the Subcommittee did not take Reuter up on his offer. Instead, they decided to seek accreditation through another avenue—the incorporation of their own homemade accrediting body. Articles of incorporation for the "North American Accrediting Agency" were drawn up, listing Subcommittee staff members as its board of directors and incorporators. In fact, the articles were identical to those drawn up earlier for Capitol Institute except for North American's purpose which was to "promote higher standards of education offered in private learning institutions" and "to promote higher standards of approval for accrediting bodies." Accordingly, upon payment of another $42 incorporation fee, along with two copies of its articles of incorporation, North American Accrediting Agency was just as legal in the District of Columbia as the equally phony Capitol Institute (U.S. Congress, House, 11 December 1985, pp. 135–136).

The "West European Accrediting Agency," which accredited the fraudulent Roosevelt University, among others, was active even during the trial of Roosevelt's creators in the fall of 1987. When an ACE staff member wrote for information about "Roosevelt University" she received—in an envelope postmarked Brussels, Belgium, on April 16, 1987—a sheet indicating that the "1A rating" for the diploma mill's accreditation meant full recognition of degrees at all levels. It was also stated that such accreditation was recognized not only in Europe but in countries on three other continents. This communique would sound good to anyone who did not know that: European universities are not "accredited" in the American sense of the term; and accredited universities in the United States are not "rated." In fact, the "university" in question did not even exist as a legal institutional entity in *any* European country.

COPA specifies a number of "Provisions for Recognition" that it considers as indicators of a quality program of accreditation (Council on Postsecondary Accreditation, July 1987). Some forty-seven such criteria are listed; the following are of particular importance when applied to an accrediting body requesting COPA recognition:

- Describes, in official public documents, its full accrediting scope, evaluative criteria, and procedures
- Is solely responsible for the final decision on accreditation of an institution or program
- Provides evidence that its policies, evaluative criteria, procedures, and evaluative decisions are accepted by the appropriate communities of interest such as educators, educational institutions, other accrediting bodies, practitioners, employers, and public agencies
- Develops and interprets its evaluative criteria to encourage institutional freedom and automony, the improvement of institutions and programs, sound educational experimentation, and constructive innovation
- Has mechanisms to provide public correction of incorrect or misleading statements about the accreditation status of an

accredited (or candidate) institution or program, the contents of reports of site visitors and/or its accrediting actions
- Makes available on request the academic and professional qualifications of individual participants in its activities, including the members of its policy and decision-making bodies and its administrative personnel
- Utilizes evaluative criteria and processes that judge (1) the appropriateness of the institutional or program purposes; (2) the adequacy of resources and organization to meet those purposes; (3) educational outcomes which indicate that those purposes are met; and (4) the reasonable assurance of continued meeting of those purposes
- Appoints site visitors using procedures developed to select visitors who are: (1) qualified by academic training, professional experience and knowledge of the accrediting process; (2) sensitive to the uniqueness of individual institutions and programs; and (3) impartial, objective, and without conflict of interest
- Provides reasonable checks and balances in its procedures to guard against: (1) accrediting an institution or program that does not meet its criteria, and (2) refusing to accredit an institution or program that does meet its criteria.

Although accreditation is not required of institutions, and participation in the process is voluntary, its uses by various organizations, constituencies, and individuals have made it almost a necessity for survival in the postsecondary education community. The federal government uses accreditation as an eligibility factor for disbursing certain funds. Many private foundations require accreditation as a prerequisite for receiving grants. Parents, prospective students, and counselors appreciate that accredited status indicates that the educational activities of an institution or program meet at least minimum standards of quality.

It is rare for an institution having COPA-recognized accreditation to accept the credit or degrees of an institution that does not have it. On this account, institutions admitting students from unaccredited institutions generally take special steps to validate credits and credentials earned.

A certain few legitimate institutions of postsecondary education do not seek COPA-recognized recognition for reasons unrelated to questions of academic quality. South Carolina's Bob Jones University at Greenville, for example, has not sought accreditation for religious reasons.

Why should institutions having accreditation by an agency recognized by COPA or the U.S. Department of Education* have, in effect, a monopoly on the award of degrees issued and generally accepted in the United States? Perhaps they should not— a possibility taken into account by at least a few professional associations that perform certification functions for members and others. The American Speech–Language–Hearing Association, for example, has recently approved guidelines for establishing the equivalence of doctoral degrees from an institution lacking COPA-recognized accreditation. The guidelines include basic eligibility criteria and statements of "critical outcomes" and "critical process elements" that will be considered in such evaluations. The Association says that if the degree in question meets its minimum criteria (as determined by an Equivalency Review Panel), the individual who earned the degree indeed may use that degree in connection with any aspect of the profession of speech–language pathology and audiology.

In summary, COPA-recognized accreditation, while highly respected generally within the higher education community in the United States, is not an infallible guarantee of quality. However, apart from such accreditation, it is very difficult for American colleges and universities to provide reliable, third-party assurance that they meet or exceed minimum standards generally accepted within the mainstream higher education community.

State governments are of little help in determining which accrediting agencies have, at best, casual standards. No state has any statutes governing the operation of accrediting bodies. In trying to sort out diploma mills from legitimate colleges and universities, the acronym "COPA" is a good indicator to watch for.

*The U.S. Department of Education does not accredit institutions, but it does have its own system of recognizing accrediting agencies. See chapter 12 for an explanation of this function.

10
State Laws:
The Baseline Defense

The great bulk of problems associated with diploma mills in the United States could be eliminated if states enacted—and enforced—appropriate laws governing the organization and administration of postsecondary education institutions. *Minimum standards* for organizations allowed to call themselves colleges and universities would be the essence of a good, fundamental law. A law should not, however, be so strict as to put the state into the business of accreditation which is a higher level function more appropriately performed by accrediting agencies.

Because it is not mentioned in the U.S. Constitution's Tenth Amendment, education is one of the powers "not delegated to the United States and not prohibited to the states." The effect of this has been that education has evolved as a state responsibility in America.

Most states now have reasonably good laws with respect

127

to postsecondary education institutions and enforce them conscientiously. Unhappily, a few states have taken their responsibilities all too lightly.

The language of regulation for postsecondary education institutions in some states is confused and open to interpretation which benefits diploma mill operators. There are no universally accepted definitions of such terms as authorization, acceptance, licensing, certification, recognition, appraisal, classification, registration, approval, chartering, or even accreditation—all of which may be used to refer to various stages of institutional organization or development. To make matters worse, some words may correctly be used in reference to entirely different things. For example, "approval" may apply to an institution's charter for organization, its degree-awarding status, or to its eligibility to receive certain federal funds.

Some kind of consistently marked pathway through this maze is essential if the relevant state laws are to be understood. *For purposes of this volume*, we will introduce definitions of these terms: (1) incorporation; (2) authorization; (3) approval (degree-granting); (4) approval (veterans' benefits); and (5) certification.* It is important to remember, however, that these terms may have quite different meanings when used in the statutes or regulations of the various states.

Incorporation. Each state has at least one incorporation law under which individuals may organize for the purpose of engaging in commerce or receiving and disbursing funds. If the organization is a nonprofit entity, the state may reserve some legal regulatory authority under laws applying to charitable trusts. Such laws may or may not have special provisions relating to colleges, universities, and theological seminaries. The same or comparable process is frequently called chartering, licensure, registration, or authorization. Incorporation means that an organization has the right to exist. Depending on other state laws, it may or may not mean that the organization is also authorized to award degrees. The administrative responsibilities for incorporation are fre-

*The terms "licensure" and "accrediting," also relevant, are defined in chapters 7 and 9, respectively.

quently assigned to a state's secretary of state or attorney general.

Authorization. In some states, the process of authorization is separate from the process of incorporation. In other states, incorporation and authorization are one and the same thing. In this volume, "authorization" is used in a generic sense to refer to state recognition that an organization has the right to exist *and* to award degrees at the most minimum acceptable level of organization and resources.

Approval (Degree-Granting). One state, California, provides an opportunity for institutions of postsecondary education to apply for and be granted official state "approval." This is considered to be a different level of recognition from authorization in that the institution must meet different standards than those only applying for minimum level "authorization." It should be emphasized that approval in California is *not* state accreditation, nor is it broadly recognized in the American higher education community as "equivalent to accreditation" under standards adhered to by accrediting agencies recognized by COPA. At the present time in California, institutions must hold "approval" status before they can apply for institutional accreditation from one of the accrediting commissions of the Western Association of Schools and Colleges (WASC). (Chapter 11 provides a complete description of "approval" status in California.)

Approval (Veterans' Benefits). Colleges and universities of every stripe hunger and thirst after federal dollars. Consequently, the government has established procedures for defending itself against gross exploitation. Each state is required by law (Title 38, U.S. Code, Section 1775(a)) to establish a "state approving agency" to certify that courses offered to veterans eligible to receive aid under the G.I. Bills are provided by an institution accredited by an agency recognized by the U.S. Department of Education.

Certification. The process of certification is conducted by a unit (usually but not always nongovernmental in nature) which grants recognition to an *individual* who has met qualifications specified by that organization. Such recognition usually means that the individual thereafter is granted permission to use a particular professional or occupational title. Certification is *voluntary* and is defined here because it may sometimes be accepted by a state as qualifying a person to be licensed to perform a particular job. For example, engineers, nurses, or psychologists may need to be "certified" by their professional associations before they can be "licensed" by a state to work in their professions. (A frequent requirement of certification is that the person who applies hold appropriate degrees from an educational institution possessing accreditation from an agency recognized by COPA or the U.S. Department of Education.)

A common diploma mill ploy is to mislead the public about its degree of acceptability under state laws. While state authorization is an important step toward providing some consumer protection, it must not be confused with accreditation where concern goes considerably beyond consumer protection to the quality of educational offerings. In some states, authorization may include little more than filing an application and paying a small fee. Thus, a phrase such as "state-authorized" does not necessarily mean that any evaluation of the educational quality has been made. It may mean only that the institution can demonstrate some fiscal responsibility and is willing to make a public disclosure of some information about itself.

Texas has a law designed to prevent misleading use of its "certificate of authorization" as representing endorsement, approval, accreditation, or any other form of recognition beyond simple authority to operate. Whenever reference is made to this certificate in publications, advertisements, or any other representations, the following statement *must be cited in its entirety*.

> The Coordinating Board, Texas College and University System has granted a Certificate of Authority to [Name of Institution] to award the degrees listed below:
>
> [Names of Degrees Must Be Listed Here]
>
> This certificate is a license to operate in the State of Texas and does not constitute accreditation; the issuance of this certificate attests only to an institution's having met the Board's minimum standards established for purposes of consumer protection under Subchapter G, Chapter 61, V.T.C.A.

A number of problems associated with diploma mill activity could be alleviated if a similar requirement were imposed by other states.

The responsibility of authorizing, approving, and otherwise regulating postsecondary education institutions generally rests with a state's department of education, state higher education board for coordination or governance, or a commission having a specific charge for this purpose. In some states, nonprofit and for-profit (proprietary) institutions may be regulated under differing laws, procedures, and even regulatory agencies. In Ohio, for example, the Ohio Board of Regents is statutorily responsible for authorizing all nonprofit collegiate instructional progams, while the State Board of School and College Registration is responsible for authorizing all proprietary college-level institutions.

In an effort to provide guidance to states in the enactment of fair and adequate laws governing the incorporation and authorization of educational institutions, the Education Commission of the States (ECS) developed model state legislation in 1973. This model legislation was put together by a task force whose membership was drawn from representatives of state government, state agencies concerned with different aspects of postsecondary education and its regulations, the U.S. Office of Education, major accrediting agencies, postsecondary education institutions (including "complex institutions"), and proprietary education.

The ECS model legislation, in essence, is not intended to facilitate or encourage massive governmental intervention into the world of education. Rather, it is intended to establish minimum standards, both academic and fiscal, that must be met if an institution is truly to function as an educational entity. Among the provisions of the model legislation are the following.

Purposes. Citizens, students, and institutions are to be protected through the state's regulatory powers against questionable, unethical, and fraudulent practices (including such practices by diploma mills).

Definitions. A broad definition of the term "postsecondary educational institution" is urged so as to include all operations and programs available to persons of post-high school age. A similar broad definition is recommended for the representative of any such institution. Accordingly, any "agent" under the legislation refers to anyone who received compensation from an institution, as well as anyone who attempts to encourage persons to attend or receive credentials.

Agency of Authorization. The model legislation is not prescriptive with respect to which agency of the state government should be designated to oversee institutional authorization, but it does suggest acceptable alternative administrative arrangements. In any event, the designated agency should have the capability and experience for using regulatory powers. Yet, it should also have "understanding and empathy for" the institutions being regulated.

Powers and Duties. Of crucial importance in the model legislation are the statements of powers and duties that the agency of authorization should have. Among such powers and duties are these:

1. To establish minimum criteria under which institutions are authorized to operate
2. To receive, investigate, and act upon applications for authorization to operate
3. To maintain a list of institutions and agents authorized to operate
4. To negotiate and enter into interstate reciprocity agreements bearing on the agency's mission
5. To receive and maintain academic records of institutions that cease operation
6. To investigate complaints.

Minimum Standards. Standards applying to institutional authorization must include consideration of the institution's ability to enable students to reach its educational objectives. They also encompass adequate, fair, and accurate information for prospective students in regard to the objectives, costs, and conditions involved.

Prohibitions. A number of practices are specifically prohibited under the model legislation. Among these is operation without state authorization. Importantly, recruiting and advertising are ruled out unless the organization is in compliance with minimum standards and related rules and regulations.

Agents Permit. Persons who "solicit or perform the services of an agent" must apply for a permit. This application is to be accompanied by evidence of the good reputation and character of the applicant. There must also be provisions for revocation of an agent's permit.

Enforcement. The best state standards are impotent unless there is adequate provision for enforcement. The model law specifies appropriate procedures for revocation of an institutional authorization or agent's permit, as well as procedures leading toward possible civil or criminal penalties.

There has been no formal update of the ECS model legislation though it is known that a number of states have since adopted (or adapted) some of its provisions. Such an updating is long overdue. For example, the advent of academic programs delivered via electronic media from out-of-state institutions is presenting problems—as well as great opportunities. Most state laws say nothing on this vital subject.

In 1987 The Center for Adult Learning and Educational Credentials of ACE conducted a survey of state governments to ascertain the present state laws governing the incorporation, authorization, and approval of degree-granting postsecondary education institutions (see Appendix D).

A number of states clearly have strong laws regulating the activities of organizations calling themselves colleges and universities. Among these states are Arizona (since January 1, 1985), Arkansas, Connecticut, District of Columbia, Illinois, Indiana, Maine, Maryland, Massachusetts, Nevada, New Jersey, New York, Ohio, Oregon, Pennsylvania, Puerto Rico, Rhode Island, Tennessee, Texas, Vermont, Washington, and West Virginia (also Wisconsin for proprietary institutions only). In the recent past, reported diploma mill sightings in most of these states are few and far between.

The Center's survey also confirms that some states still have relatively weak laws—or none at all as in Hawaii where state government officials do not, as a matter of policy, even respond to inquiries on the subject. Other states with weak laws include Idaho, Iowa, Louisiana, Missouri, Montana, Nebraska, New Mexico, Oklahoma, South Dakota, Utah, Wisconsin (except for proprietary institutions), and Wyoming. Many inquiries or complaints about alleged diploma mills have been recorded from some of these states.

States having weak laws are more likely to attract would-be diploma mill operators, though by no means all of those states appear to have such an affliction. In testimony before the Pepper Subcommittee, diploma mill operator Anthony Geruntino cited five states (Arizona, Hawaii, Utah, Wyoming, and Missouri) as particularly favorable at that time for casual acceptance of new educational organizations (U.S. Congress, House, 11 December 1988, p. 50). He founded Southwestern University, one of his big moneymakers, in the State of Arizona which at the time lacked any pertinent regulatory legislation (a defect happily remedied since).

Arizona's turnabout probably could not have been accomplished had it not been for an explosive series of newspaper articles that exposed the rampant diploma production under the old laws. Michael Satchell, a reporter for the *Clarion-Ledger* in Jackson, Mississippi, proudly earned a "fraudulent" Ph.D. in psychology and counseling from an Arizona diploma mill while doing an investigative story (Satchell, 1984). But his record, impressive though it is, pales in comparison with that of reporters Jerry Seper and Richard Robertson of the *Arizona Republic* in Phoenix. They not only acquired the degrees, but within two weeks created the university that could do it. They also had a "prestigious" accrediting agency to provide added lustre. And it was all done in full compliance with Arizona laws under which universities could be "chartered and recognized." Incorporation took less than five minutes; no questions were asked. The total cost was $100 (Seper and Robertson, 1983).

An added major difficulty for state officials, as well as accrediting agency representatives, has been the practice among colleges and universities of establishing branches in other states. A significant share of these branches are located on military bases. In the absence of adequate resources including competent faculty and effective administrative support, even a legitimate university program can go awry. For the diploma

Ohio's statutes governing higher education institutions are tough which is why Anthony Geruntino was careful to conduct "educational" activities in Arizona rather than from this location at 4214-4216 East Broad Street in Columbus. However, at this site "Southwestern University" had its related national program office, evaluation center and association, and corporate finance center, according to the FBI. Geruntino was eventually arrested and pled guilty to charges of wire and mail fraud. In 1985, he was sentenced to five years in prison and was fined $5,000. (Courtesy of Federal Bureau of Investigation.)

mill operator, the arrangement can be ideal if it removes the operation from official scrutiny in the state where the organization is domiciled.

State regulatory agencies ordinarily assume that the "site state" will oversee all education-related activities within its borders. This assumption is sometimes erroneous and can result in trouble. A state agency may act as an effective policeman in its own jurisdiction while allowing organizations domiciled there to exploit citizens of other states or even foreign countries. For example, by declaring itself unauthorized to regulate actions that occur outside its borders, the California Private Postsecondary Education Division may unintentionally be exporting problems to its counterpart agencies in other states and foreign countries.

What happens if a state decides to enact tough new statutes and then works to enforce them? According to the 1977 report issued by the Association for Continuing Higher Education (ACHE) special committee, results can be encouraging. At that time, the states of Florida and Indiana—once havens for legal diploma mill operation—were reported to have corrected at least the most blatant abuses. Under a recently enacted law, Florida had closed down at least one hundred highly questionable institutions. Contempt proceedings were initiated against another organization for violation of a permanent injunction that had been issued in 1972 (Association for Continuing Higher Education, 1977, p. 15).

Progress against similar problems in Indiana was reported by Joseph A. Clark of the Indiana Private School Accreditation Commission (a state agency) before the U.S. House of Representatives Committee on Education and Labor and the Committee on Government Operations. In 1960, according to Clark, his state had 25 percent of all the diploma mills operating in the United States. By 1971, the state had a new and stringent state law that resulted in 276 illegal or inadequate organizations being put out of business by 1974 (Association for Continuing Higher Education, 1977, p. 15).

Missouri's laws are still weak but even the modest improvement in 1984 that established minimal state regulation had its effect. Between 1984 and 1987, at least forty-eight of sixty organizations lacking COPA-recognized accreditation ceased to operate.

Tight authorization laws may also result in some curious organizational anomalies. A team reviewing the academic programs of a Canadian institution authorized in the province of Quebec, for example, found the organizational structure there to be ephemeral, almost nonexistent. The real business of the institution was transacted in the neighboring province of Ontario which has a very tough law governing organization of colleges and universities. Apparently the institution's owners maintained the Quebec entity as a front to sidestep Ontario's tougher laws.

A word of caution is in order for those who might relax after noticing that a particular state has what may be called relatively tough laws governing the organization and administration of educational institutions. There may be important exemptions for some institutions (e.g., those having religious missions or those organized on a private, nonprofit basis). Or it may be more difficult to start a diploma mill legally in a state, but a grandfather clause in the new law may permit an existing diploma mill to continue operating as it had in the past.

Enforcement, too, may be unevenly applied depending upon the political climate in the state as well as on staffing patterns. In reviewing survey forms returned to ACE, it is clear that in some states, governmental agencies believe themselves to have a staff that does not have the skills or is too small to accomplish effective enforcement.

Relatively weak laws should not necessarily be interpreted to mean that a state is a mecca for diploma mills. In some states, a tough-minded enforcement agency can effectively discourage diploma mills even if statutory weapons against them are limited. Also, effective leadership on the part of a state's higher education and state governmental community can be a deterrent to questionable educational activities.

Regulations can also be weapons in the hands of executive branch officials determined to keep diploma mills under control. In Rhode Island, for example, no institution can grant degrees without authorization from the state's Board of Governors for Higher Education. The regulations developed by the Board specify rigorous criteria that will be applied before any institution receives such authorization. Broadly written statutes interpreted by strict regulations become as effective as more tightly written statutes not accompanied by such regulations.

In the end, sound legislation at the state level is the first line of defense against unscrupulous diploma mill operators. But legislation by itself is insufficient. A well-equipped enforcement agency and a public mood that will support its efforts are also needed.

11

California: A Very Special Case

It is no accident that the majority of questionable educational entities in the United States are, or have been, located in the state of California. California now has statutes governing the authorization and approval of educational institutions that are arguably better than some of those that were replaced. But these changes came too late. Previous laws were weak and, in effect, encouraged development of diploma mills because the laws gave them a certain legitimacy in the eyes of the public. In this environment, diploma mills thrived, and grew strong politically, as numerous elected and appointed state officials can attest.

Thousands of people in California, in other states, and in other countries hold degrees from extremely questionable California institutions, many of which continue to exist. These organizations with their lobbyists, political action committees, and administrators posing as "innovators" constitute a powerful lobby against corrective action.

The statutes causing the trouble are Sections 94310(c) and 94310(b) of the earlier and current California Education Code. The original (c) statute authorized an organization to award degrees with only the barest semblance of an academic or financial framework. The organization was merely required to file an annual affidavit of "full disclosure" describing its curriculum, faculty, facilities, course of study and degrees offered. Affidavits submitted by the organization also had to state the names of officers and board members and certify that its assets for educational purposes were at least $50,000. A site visit by the Private Postsecondary Education Division was conducted. However, the state's Superintendent of Public Instruction could deny or withdraw authorization to operate only if the affidavits were inaccurate.

In practice, this provision became a national joke as notorious diploma mills qualified in large numbers to organize and prosper in California. Some idea on the quality of academic muscle of certain of these institutions is provided in the case of one state-authorized institution that, as it applied for reauthorization for 1986-1987, reported a student–faculty ratio of 450:1. All was not lost, however. In the same letter, they said they were anticipating improving this to 400:1 during the next year. As a comparison, the ratio of full-time equivalent enrollment to full-time instructional staff at all accredited institutions in 1982 was 16.4:1, according to ACE's *1986-87 Fact Book on Higher Education*.

Another provision of the old California statutes also caused trouble that lingers on today. Section 94310(b) enabled the Department of Education's Private Postsecondary Education Division to "approve" specific degree programs at any authorized institution. Such an approval process involved a state-supervised review of a degree program which might result in official state "approval" of such a program. In practice, many organizations that gained such approval for specific degree programs sought to equate it in the eyes of the public with

COPA-recognized or U.S. Department of Education recognized institutional accreditation.

Also, approval was by no means a guarantee of quality. For example, the attorney general's office in a southern state notes the case of a resident in his state who obtained a Ph.D. in psychology from a California institution holding "approved" status under the old law. (This Ph.D. was awarded, it is alleged, after the person submitted a seventeen page dissertation and defended it for thirty minutes on the telephone.)

Under the new California statutes, there are six categories of recognition the state may use in designating institutions to issue, confer, or award degrees. The Education Code references for these are shown in the following table, along with references for those statutes that were replaced.

CALIFORNIA'S SIX CATEGORIES FOR INSTITUTIONAL DESIGNATION

Designation	Formerly	Presently
U.S. Department of Education-Recognized Accreditation or Accreditation by the California Committee of Bar Examiners (In-State Institutions)	94310(a)	94310.1(a)
U.S. Department of Education-Recognized Accreditation (Out-of-State Institutions)	(None)	94310.1(b)
State-Approved Institutions	94310(b)	94310.2
State-Authorized Institutions	94310(c)	94310.3
State-Authorized "Schools of Theology"	94310(d)	94310.4
Exempted Religious Institutions	94303(b)	94303(b)

There is a lack of awareness and much confusion about

what each of these designations means—a situation that a
number of questionable institutions operating in California
have been quick to exploit as they attempt to recruit students
in states other than California or in foreign countries. Sorting
everything out is not all that easy, but here are the essentials
of these often misunderstood California statutes.

Accreditation (94310.1 (a) and 94310.1 (b))

An "accredited institution" operating under Section
94310.1(a) is one based in California which has accreditation
by a national accrediting agency recognized by the U.S. Department of Education, the Western Association of Schools
and Colleges (WASC), or by the Committee of Bar Examiners
for the State of California.

California also makes provision for accredited institutions domiciled in other states to conduct off-campus programs
in California under Section 94310.1 (b). Before this status is
granted, the Private Postsecondary Education Division reviews the applying institution through a process that is co-
ordinated with accrediting agencies located in the institution's
home region.

State Approval (94310.2)

The Superintendent of Public Instruction in California
may designate an authorized institution as "approved" if it
meets "recognized and accepted standards" for awarding degrees. Such approval is given by the Superintendent after
review of the institution by a committee consisting of representatives from both accredited and state-approved institutions. The new law also makes provision for an institution
to be designated a "Candidate for Institutional Approval."
Under the new law, the programmatic approval designation
was eliminated and replaced with a designation of full institutional approval.

There is no requirement or necessarily an expectation
that an authorized institution "progress" to approved and then
accredited status. However, the accrediting commissions of

the Western Association of Schools and Colleges require that an institution first hold approved status under California law before they will accept their applications for "candidacy for accreditation" status.

Just what is involved in obtaining approval status from the California Superintendent of Public Instruction? Prior to submitting a formal application for approval, the applicant undergoes a "self-readiness review and assessment" with guidance provided by a consultant from the Private Postsecondary Education Division. After examination, the consultant provides the institution with a written report of readiness findings that includes an assessment of the institution's chances of obtaining approval if it submits a formal application. Revisions that might make the report more acceptable to the Superintendent may be suggested. This is, of course, a professional judgment, not a legal decision. An institution may proceed toward applying for full approval, if it chooses to do so, even in the absence of a positive report from the Division's consultant.

After the institution's application is submitted, the next step is an on-site review by a visiting committee appointed by the Superintendent. The size of the team varies depending on the number and type of programs offered. Members are selected from a pool that may include persons nominated by the institution undergoing review. Any slate of nominees from the applying institution must be educators from institutions that are either accredited or approved under California law.

The committee conducts its review and assessment and drafts a report of its findings and recommendations. The Committee may recommend: (1) approval; (2) candidate for approval status; or (3) disapproval. An appeals procedure is provided which may be used by organizations whose applications have been disapproved.

An institution holding approved status in California may apply for additional review and assessment of programs it may want to add to those approved earlier. In this event, another self-readiness review and assessment is done and a site visit is conducted by a state consultant. The findings and recommendations are then submitted to the Superintendent of Public Instruction who grants either "conditional program approval" or disapproves the application. Review by a visiting committee resulting in full approval (or disapproval) of the new program occurs one year later or upon graduation of students, whichever comes first. In order to retain approved status, an institution must undergo reapproval review, generally every three years.

How is the new law regarding approval status faring as a guardian of academic quality? Certain aspects of the law's implementation are troubling to observers who had hoped to stem California's disproportionate contribution to the diploma mill problem. Much of the criticism arises from the claim by some approved institutions that they hold "approval equivalent to accreditation." Such claims are based upon language in the statutes which directs the Superintendent to determine that the curriculum of approved institutions "is consistent in quality with curricula offered by appropriate established accredited institutions." The statute also notes that "the course for which the degree is granted achieves its professed or claimed academic objective for higher education, with verifiable evidence of academic achievement comparable to that required of graduates of other recognized schools accredited by an appropriate accrediting Commission recognized by the United States Department of Education or the Committee of Bar Examiners for the State of California."

Approval, however, *is not* accreditation. While an institution may qualify to operate under California law either by obtaining accreditation via a COPA-recognized (or U.S. Department of Education-recognized) accrediting entity or by obtaining approval under the state-sponsored process, the two processes are different. Furthermore, the achievement of accreditation brings important dimensions of recognition by other accredited institutions that may not ordinarily be achieved by institutions that have state approval.

Jonathan Brown, Vice President of the Association of Independent California Colleges and Universities, has noted the "considerable concern" expressed by accredited institutions that the characterization of approval as "comparable" to accreditation is "misleading and inappropriate." In a 1987 issue paper entitled, "Accreditation and Licensure—How Does the State Assure Itself of Quality Control in Higher Education?" Brown suggests that the "ultimate test of the statute's call for comparability is whether an institution's credits would be readily transferable to an accredited institution." The same language, Brown asserts, may create the possibility that a state system of accreditation might be established (Brown, 1987).

Accounts of activities at some approved institutions are troubling. The visitation report for one institution seeking approval under California law (and eventually attaining it) points up real discrepancies between the announced philosophy of the institution and the practical applications of it. The institution had a stated educational philosophy apparently centering on futurism and the organic relationships between parts and wholes. But the connections between this philosophy and what happened in the instructional programs seemed tenuous at best. Indeed, faculty members interviewed seemed unaware of what the applications might be. Students who were interviewed could not recall any instance in which the institution's philosophical concepts were introduced to undergird their educational programs.

Faculty members at the same institution, some 40 percent of whom held degrees from their employer, seemed to lack understanding of what levels of knowledge were required in order to qualify for the various degrees. There was little evidence of formal assessment of the prior learning that had been accepted for credit and much of the work accepted for credit appeared to have little or no relation to the degree to which it was applied. Moreover, several dissertations appeared to have been written before the individuals were enrolled at the institution—an unusual practice to say the least.

Assuming these portions of the committee's report are true and accurate, would it be possible that such an institution could function legitimately given the same combination of management and resources? There is at least room for skepticism here.

In 1987 one of the authors requested permission of the Private Postsecondary Education Division to participate as an observer in an "approval" site visit. The institution in question was one about which ACE has received many inquiries and reports of complaints. This request was denied by the Division's acting director after an objection was raised by the institution undergoing review. This action is not one that inspires confidence in an era where openness in most transactions involving governmental agencies is the expected norm.

If there are problems from an academic perspective, such concerns may not be shared by some officials at key agencies in the state government structure. A spokesperson for the California Department of Education's Private Postsecondary Education Division reports that degrees awarded by institutions holding "approved" status are being recognized by most California professional and occupational licensing boards (e.g., law, psychology, engineering). The same degree programs also are qualifying for approval for veterans benefits provided under the G.I. Bill (Title 38, U.S. Code).

State Authorization (94310.3)

In order to offer degrees in the state of California, any educational institution must at least be authorized under Section 94310.3. This designation means that the Superintendent of Public Instruction has determined, after review of the institution by a visiting committee, that the institution meets minimum standards for existence as an educational institution offering degrees at the postsecondary level.

Some institutions elect to continue under this basic authorization designation and never seek "approved" or "accredited" status as is their right under California law. Authorization may not extend for more than five years and may be issued for a shorter period of time.

In conducting site visits at institutions currently authorized or newly applying for Section 94310.3 status, the Private Postsecondary Education Division visiting committee now uses a detailed questionnaire containing 111 standards called for by law. Questions are arranged in twelve general categories: (1) institutional objectives, (2) means of achieving the objectives, (3) curriculum, (4) methods of instruction, (5) faculty with qualifications, (6) physical facilities, (7) administrative personnel, (8) educational record-keeping procedures, (9) tuition and fee schedule and tuition refund schedule, (10) admissions standards, scholastic regulations, and graduation requirements, (11) degrees offered, and (12) financial stability.

Not everyone, however, is happy about the performance of some institutions having authorized status. While acknowledging that the new statute is having the effect of "weeding out marginal institutions," the California Postsecondary Education Commission staff in a 1987 report indicates that it has "both procedural concerns and concerns that the standards which the law was intended to strengthen still have some significant weaknesses." One procedural concern is "the length of the process and the immense amount of time and energy it consumes."

The Commission staff notes that at some institutions "instructional procedures" provide for "nothing more than mailing a textbook and final exam to a student and grading the final exam." Sometimes the exam may be graded by a member of the administration, not the faculty. Also, records examined by the Commission indicate that most of the interaction between mentors and students is "procedural, having little to do with the content of the course."

While these criticisms need to be taken seriously, there is no evidence that the newly implemented authorization process in California is seriously deficient. One of the authors participated as an observer in the authorization site visit at a new institution organizing in Southern California in December 1986. The process, as observed, appeared to be satisfactory for assuring appropriate review of institutional structure and integrity at the most minimal level as required by law.

Authorization to Award Degrees in Theology or Religion (94310.4)

A special category of authorization applies only to institutions awarding degrees in theology or religion in the state of California. This designation is given by the Superintendent of Public Instruction to such institutions after they have filed affidavits spelling out institutional objectives and proposed methods of achieving them. Also required is information about curriculum, instruction, faculty with qualifications, physical facilities, administrative personnel, educational record-keeping procedures, tuition and fee schedule, tuition refund schedule, scholastic regulations, degrees to be conferred, graduation requirements, and financial stability.

The state is careful to keep itself out of the business of judging curriculum content in this category. The thrust of this section in the law is to assure the public that the institution has the resources to deliver what it promises and that the degrees offered are not thinly disguised degrees in liberal arts or subjects other than theology and religion.

In the language of the law, a school of theology is one "in which the education is restricted primarily to courses or curriculum in theology or ministry and other education or instruction directly related to theology or ministry, the content of which is not necessarily limited to the principles of any particular church or denomination. The title of any such degree must include specific language that identifies the degree as one of theology or ministry" (California Administrative Code, Titles, Section 18801 (f) as stated in California "Authorization of Degree-Granting Schools of Theology," December 1984).

Exempted Religious Institutions (94303 (b))

Not all degree-granting institutions in California are covered by the Education Code. Specifically, a religious exemption from provisions of the Private Postsecondary Education Act (Section 94303(b)) may be granted to a "nonprofit institution owned, controlled, and operated and maintained by a bona fide church or religious denomination if the education is limited to instructions in the principles of that church or denomination, or to courses offered pursuant to Section 2789 of the Business and Professions Code, and the diploma or degree is limited to evidence of completion of that education, and the meritorious recognition upon which any honorary degree is conferred is limited to the principles of that church or denomination." Institutions covered by this statute may award all levels of degrees, including the Ph.D.

The intent here is to exempt institutions that are designed as merely mechanisms for implementing the religious mission of the sponsoring church. However, the missions of some churches are broad, and it is not always clear just where doctrine ends and becomes education of a type that should be regulated under provisions of the education code. It is at least possible that this exemption could be used by unscrupulous individuals to circumvent laws governing other degree-granting institutions.

Considered in the broadest context, how well are these new laws that define and regulate the various categories of degree-granting institutions in California working? While it is premature to make any comprehensive judgment, some indicator straws are in the wind.

When it enacted the new amendments to the authorization statute in 1984, the California Legislature attempted to correct—or at least ameliorate—the more gross problems spawned by its earlier law. No grandfather provision was provided that exempted any institutions holding authorization under the earlier law from provisions of the new one. The Legislature instead specified that all nonaccredited institutions authorized under the old law must prepare for and receive a site visit conducted by a team appointed by the Private Postsecondary Education Division. Such visits had to be done by June 30, 1987. Institutions that did not meet the minimum standards or failed to file the necessary papers were to have their authorization withdrawn.

There have, however, been some problems in implementing this requirement. For one thing, the camel is already in the tent and has taken possession of a good bit of living space. Political pressures, generally subtle, are sometimes quite difficult for the Private Postsecondary Education Division to resist. At times the staff appears to have been worn down by continuous resubmissions of applications for authorization or approval—each of them outwardly responsive to the Division's previously expressed concerns. It is not always easy to determine whether the announced changes in plans are real or simply cosmetic.

The involved appeals processes open to applicants for authorization or approval under California law may, at times, act as a deterrent to state regulatory agencies as they contemplate the expense and stress of such procedures. As an alternative, it becomes easier to work closely with an institution applying for authorization or approval to see that the application is expressed in the best possible way and that it is backed by some semblance of academic resources. This approach, while noble in spirit, will only work when the institution undergoing review is operated by people of ability and integrity. When this process is used with institutions owned or operated by irresponsible or unscrupulous individuals, the exercise becomes one of erecting an academic facade—or a house built upon the sand, as the Bible puts it. The appearance of quality may be there, but there is no foundation or real substance.

Nonaccredited institutions in California are by no means voiceless in the halls of state government. Their political visibility is evidenced in the make-up of the state-authorized Council for Private Postsecondary Educational Institutions which is charged with advising the Superintendent of Public Instruction in establishing policy under the statutes. This body also must establish a process, in cooperation with the Superintendent, for developing and promoting rules and regulations governing private postsecondary education. The Superintendent of Public Instruction and also the Senate Rules Committee and the Speaker of the Assembly are obligated under the law to appoint representatives of nonaccredited, degree-granting institutions to the Council. This obligation is not surprising since representatives of nonaccredited institutions helped to write the new California statutes and in the process reaffirmed their ties to the legislature and other political sectors.

At the time the new statutes took effect on July 1, 1985, California had 168 institutions authorized under Section 94310.3 of the Education Code. As of June 30, 1987, fifty-eight organizations held official status as degree-granting institutions under the same Section including twelve out-of-state accredited institutions with instructions to file under another section of the law. Among the other applicants were institutions awarding degrees in diverse subjects ranging from acupuncture, psychotherapy, and technology to liberal arts, theology, and law. Sixty-one organizations had either ceased business or been closed by the Superintendent of Public Instruction. Another sixty-seven institutions filed under other sections of the law (e.g., religious exemption, accreditation status, or school of theology).

When the new law was enacted, sixty-seven institutions held "approved" status for at least one degree under the old law. As of June 30, 1987, forty-one of those institutions had been granted "approval" under the more rigorous strictures of the new laws. A total of eighteen additional reviews were completed with action pending final decision. Two new institutions that filed for approval were approved during the same period.

Out of twelve organizations that had "candidate approval" under the old California law, only one had received full approval under the 94310(b) provisions as of June 30, 1987. During the same period, eleven institutions went from 94310(c) (authorized) status to 94310 (b) (approved) status. A number of institutions signaled their intention to apply for approval but were counseled not to do so by the Private Postsecondary Education Division staff.

In summary, it can certainly be said that, while not perfect, the new California laws governing authorization (Section 94310.3) afford a degree of consumer protection that the old laws did not. However, most observers close to the community of higher education institutions are considerably less sanguine about both the substance and the implementation of the new laws governing approval (Section 94310.2).

The jury is still out in its consideration of the new California statutes governing institutions of postsecondary education. Both the law itself and the enforcement mechanisms are on trial. Because of the proclivity of many California institutions to recruit students at locations far outside the state boundaries, virtually the whole world—literally—will be affected by what happens.

12

The Federal Government: A Limited Role

As chapter 10 discussed, education is a responsibility of state governments in the United States. But this does not mean that the federal government is disinterested or that it takes no action affecting the quality of postsecondary education provided to American citizens.

Five federal government agencies have responsibilities bearing on the diploma mill problem: the Department of Education, the Federal Bureau of Investigation (FBI), the U.S. Postal Inspection Service, the Federal Trade Commission (FTC), and the Department of State.

The U.S. Office of Education, immediate predecessor agency to today's Cabinet-level Department of Education, had a long history of wrestling with the problem of diploma mills. While it never had regulatory authority, the office was established in 1867 in part as an effort to sort out the chaos then, as now, prevailing in the education community about what type of organization could call itself a college or university (Reid, 1964, p. 176).

For a time, beginning in 1910, the Office published a list of "approved schools," but this task proved formidable. Who was to decide what criteria were to be used in determining which institutions could be listed? Faced with a hornet's nest, President William Howard Taft wisely concluded that the federal government should get out of the business of publishing a list of approved schools. Taft's successor, Woodrow Wilson, was pressured to reissue the list, but he too concluded that the obstacles were too great (Reid, 1964, p. 181).

The idea lay dormant until 1959 when then Secretary of Health, Education, and Welfare Arthur S. Flemming decided to face the problem head on. He called a news conference to announce his intentions. Noting that degree mills had become "a blight on the American educational scene," Flemming put the resources of his department to work at finding a solution to the problem (Reid, 1964, p. 10).

Some months later, the Secretary released a list of "degree mills." Some twenty-two organizations in nine states were shown as "active" on the list; each institution had been visited and investigated by a member of the Secretary's staff. Another four organizations were shown as "inactive," and eleven were listed as "chartered in the United States but active abroad" (Reid, 1964, pp 11–12). The list was maintained and periodically updated by the Office for a time, but has since been discontinued, for both financial and legal reasons.

The Office of Education's successor, the Cabinet-level Department of Education, again in 1986 considered developing a list of diploma mills, perhaps in cooperation with ACE which also saw the need. But the idea was dropped once again, primarily because of the high risks of legal liability or, in the absence of liability, excessive legal expenses.

Instead the Department of Education is relying on the quality control functions of accreditation. The Department has concentrated upon developing and maintaining a list of national accrediting bodies and state agencies as it is required to under Title 34, U.S. Code, Section 603.3 (U.S. Department of Education, October 1986). With few exceptions, postsecondary education institutions may not qualify for federal funds unless they are accredited by an agency that has qualified for inclusion on this list. A major responsibility of the Department's Division of Eligibility and Certification is to review applications submitted by accrediting agencies wishing to be included on this list. The process is not one of peer review. Rather, staff members in the Division's Office of Higher Education Management Services review requests for recognition submitted by the various accrediting agencies against criteria that have been developed for such evaluation. Staff recommendations are considered by the National Advisory Committee on Accreditation and Evaluation which, in turn, makes recommendations to the Secretary of Education.

Because having recognized accreditation is essential before an organization can secure federal funds, the Department of Education sometimes finds itself under pressure to recognize accrediting agencies that have not been able to secure recognition by COPA. To date, the Department has been quite successful in resisting these pressures which means that for most practical purposes, its list of "Nationally Recognized Accrediting Agencies and Associations" is virtually identical to the membership of COPA.

At present, both COPA and Department of Education recognize the fourteen postsecondary institutional accrediting bodies, including the six regional commissions and the five national commissions which accredit specialized institutions (e.g., Bible colleges, graduate theological schools, trade and technical schools, private business schools, and home study institutions). Both of them also recognize thirty-two specialized accrediting bodies. As of May 6, 1987, eight others are recognized by COPA alone. The Department of Education recognizes seventeen specialized accrediting bodies which are either not eligible or have not applied for COPA recognition.

Institutions having COPA- and/or U.S. Department of Education- recognized accreditation do not have a monopoly in the realm of obtaining federal government program eligibility. There is an alternative which is defined in Chapter 20, U.S. Code, Title 34, Section 1141(a). The provisions of this alternative allow the Department to certify that an institution not accredited by a recognized entity is eligible if it "is an institution whose credits are accepted, on transfer, by not less than three institutions which are so accredited, for credit on the same basis as if transferred from an institution so accredited."

This "three-institutional-certification" method of meeting eligibility requirements, which has come to be known as the "3IC Method," was originally designed to assist institutions providing instruction in fields not served by an appropriate accrediting body. By the early 1970s, the 3IC method had been discovered by a number of questionable institutions not qualified for COPA-recognized accreditation. Then in the absence of tight controls by the Office of Education, many of these organizations were accepted and the list grew to a high of almost 120 institutions. This situation was seen and largely corrected by the Office (later Department) of Education. The 3IC list was reviewed and extensively pruned to remove a number of institutions, so that by early 1987, the list included only forty-two institutions.

Many of the institutions on the 3IC list are Hebrew teacher schools that do not currently qualify for accreditation as theological seminaries under criteria specified by the Accrediting Commission of the Association of Advanced Rabbinical and Talmudic Schools (AARTS), a COPA member. The inability of Hebrew teacher institutions to qualify for accreditation has nothing to do with the absence of academic quality in most cases. Rather, it stems from the Jewish tradition of limiting theological education in seminaries to men. The Hebrew teacher schools, which largely enroll women, have no religious accrediting agency to which they can apply.

In the recent past, the Department of Education experienced great pressure to loosen its procedures under the 3IC method so that more institutions not having COPA- or U.S. Department of Education- recognized accreditation could qualify. Diploma mill alumni and students have been in touch with their representatives and senators, some of whom have endeavored to get the Department of Education to be less circumspect in granting eligibility via the 3IC route. Fortunately, these pressures have been largely unproductive to date.

There was some sentiment in favor of removing the 3IC provision entirely from the Higher Education Act when it was reauthorized in 1986. On the surface, this change had a certain appeal from the perspective of quality control in higher education. A more reflective view is that 3IC is a needed safety valve in that it defuses the argument that COPA-recognized or U.S. Department of Education-recognized accreditation constitutes a near-monopoly in accreditation that works against the public interest. The 3IC method has also proved to be a realistic alternative for those institutions that do not wish to get generally accepted acccreditation. There is no logic in denying eligibility for federal funds to these institutions when there is no evidence that their lack of accreditation stems from academic insufficiencies.

The FBI and the U.S. Postal Inspection Service have authority to investigate violations and potential violations of the federal mail fraud statute (18 U.S. Code, Section 1341). This statute essentially makes it a federal crime (punishable by five years in jail and/or a $1,000 fine) to use the mail with intent to defraud. In addition, the FBI and the Postal Inspection Service can and do investigate cases of wire fraud (18 U.S. Code, Section 1343). Other statutes that may be used include 18 U.S. Code, Section 1342 (Fictitious Name and Address) and 18 U.S. Code, Section 1345 (Injunctions Against Fraud). The Postal Inspection Service also enforces a civil statute (39 U.S. Code, Section 3005). This provision relates to false representation in the conduct of a "scheme or device" for obtaining money or property by means of false advertising.

The FBI's "Dipscam" project, located in its regional office at Charlotte, North Carolina, is the nerve center of the Bureau's continuing pursuit of diploma mill fraud.

The Postal Inspection Service role is exemplified by their actions in the case of "Roosevelt University," which was not affiliated in any way with the legitimate Roosevelt University in Chicago. In August 1981, a letter from a resident of Thailand was referred to ACE's Office on Educational Credit and

Credentials. This individual had been in correspondence with an organization calling itself "Roosevelt University" which used as its address a legitimate, privately owned mail-receiving and mail-forwarding business located on Post Street in San Francisco.

Brochures accompanying the correspondence offered bachelor's, master's, and doctoral degrees for $780, $850, and $950 respectively. They also listed forty-eight individual degrees covering numerous fields of study, and offered "any" additional degree a person might want to apply for, except degrees in medicine and dentistry. The only requirement, besides the fee, was the submission of a brief resume of the applicant's education and work experience.

In its appeal to a foreign audience, "U.S. Education Service," which identified itself as "the agent in your country for Roosevelt University," stated it would correct the English and rewrite the resume as necessary before sending it to the parent organization. The Service even promised to back-date the applicant's degree to any date as far back as 1940, and the applicant was instructed to specify the desired date on the application form.

In addition, prospective applicants were told they would receive a basic university transcript at no extra charge, which would list the units (course credit hours), but would not include any information about how those units were "earned." Purchasers of these mail order degrees were led to believe that the degrees and transcripts would help them attain a successful, professional career in any desired field of employment.

On June 2, 1982, in response to requests from the ACE and others, the U.S. Postal Inspection Service stopped the sale of "Roosevelt" degrees through the San Francisco Post Office. The False Representation Order that was issued required the San Francisco Postmaster to return to the senders all mail addressed to the U.S. Education Service containing orders for mail order degrees.

This action was hardly the end of the university that bore the name of two American presidents, however. In typical diploma mill fashion, "Roosevelt University" continued to operate from various postal boxes around the world until 1987 when its owners were finally brought to justice at the initiative of the FBI (see Chapter 6).

The Postal Inspection Service has had notable successes, too. On January 15, 1987, it brought charges against one Ronald F. Hollander of Andover, Massachusetts. Hollander allegedly provided fraudulent credentials to the Massachusetts Board of Registration of Psychology and subsequently claimed to be a licensed psychologist with a doctoral degree from Rutgers, The State University of New Jersey. Hollander allegedly forged diplomas, supervision and collaboration reference forms, and a New Jersey Board of Psychological Examiners license. From 1977 to the date of indictment, he treated patients in Massachusetts, purporting to provide services of a person trained with a doctoral degree in the field of psychology and received payments via the U.S. mail of more than $500,000.

The FTC has no mission-related concern with the quality of American educational institutions. It does, however, have a legal responsibility (15 U.S. Code, Section 41-58) to enforce trade practice rules and to initiate complaint proceedings against organizations which disregard these rules, especially as they relate to restraint of trade and false and misleading advertising that is a part of interstate commerce. Unlike the FBI, the Postal Service, or other federal agencies, the FTC can compel diploma mills to refund money received as part of illegal actions. While the FTC has taken no action on any complaint involving diploma mills since the early 1970s, it is legally empowered to do so at its option. Such complaints may be reported to any of the FTC's ten regional offices or to its headquarters in Washington, D.C.

The U.S. Department of State has no systematic method for counting or determining the nature of the many inquiries its personnel receive concerning American educational institutions of questionable quality. Departmental officials are aware, however, of a number of instances in which foreign nationals have been deceived by unscrupulous diploma mill operators.

Three federal agencies, the FBI, the U.S. Postal Inspection Service, and the FTC play (or may play) key roles in the control of criminal activity involving diploma mill operation. And, while the U.S. Department of Education has no direct responsibilities for quality control in postsecondary education, its responsibility for developing and maintaining a list of recognized accrediting agencies makes it an indirect influence on the nature and scope of diploma mill activity.

13
Transcripts and Assorted Sundries

A host of activities related to the mass production and award of diplomas may also be conducted by organizations in the business of fraud or deception in higher education. These include: counterfeit or invalid transcripts; transcript "verification"; educational or career counseling; honorary doctorates; false certification; letters of recommendation; dissertations and term papers; sale of class rings or other jewelry; and publication of misleading directories of academic institutions.

Transcript Fraud

Two sorts of fraud or deception involve academic transcripts. The first is the practice of creating and issuing a transcript recording alleged academic achievement at a phony or grossly marginal college or university. The second is the

counterfeiting or altering of a transcript originally issued by
a legitimate college or university.

The "transcript mill" functions in about the same way as
its more generally recognized cousin that issues diplomas. To
back up the diploma, a transcript is generated. The usual
practice is simple enough. Transcripts can be purchased which
show almost any type of academic record. Sometimes, the
higher the grade, the higher the price, although it is often
recommended that a student not show "all A's," because such
outstanding achievement might be looked upon with suspicion
by a college registrar or potential employer. Sometimes cum
laude, magna cum laude, and summa cum laude, or other types
of honors are available—also for a price.

The heart and soul of the transcript fraud business is,
however, in the realm of the second category, the counterfeiting or altering of a transcript issued by a legitimate college
or university.

At the 1986 annual meeting of the American Association
of Collegiate Registrars and Admissions Officers (AACRAO),
Edward B. Gross spoke about fraudulent documents in professional schools. Gross should know. He is Manager of Transcript Processing for the Division of Student Services of the
Association of American Medical Colleges which operates a
centralized application service for more than 80 percent of
American medical schools. Along with some 30,000 applications, the organization receives between 75,000 and 80,000
academic transcripts per year.

Forged or altered transcripts are often difficult to un-
cover, according to Gross, especially if they are the products
of insiders in a registrar's office or any office having charge
of official documents, papers, seals, or computer systems.
Cruder jobs tend to be turned out by applicants who "doctor"
a transcript that is in their possession.

After heading an office that has processed more than
750,000 transcripts over a period of ten years, Gross offered
guidelines for checking transcript authenticity. These suggestions and others drawn from the experience of collegiate
registrars are contained in a 1987 publication entitled, "Mis-

representation in the Marketplace: Recognizing Fraudulent Credentials" published by AACRAO.

Designed specifically for people who use educational records for employment, financial aid, promotion, and the like, the publication specifies procedures for determining if an institution maintains a legitimate academic program. The manual further outlines the types of documents used by most colleges and universities to verify an individual's educational background and indicates the degree to which each may be protected against unauthorized alterations and reproduction. The publication also explains the role of the document recipient in assuring the security and confidentiality of all educational statements while they are being used and in identifying records' fraud.

A comparable view of transcript fraud was presented to the Pepper Subcommittee. In a statement prepared for the Congressional hearing, Dr. Bruce T. Shutt, President (1985–1986) of the AACRAO and Associate Vice President for Student Affairs and Registrar at the University of Georgia, Athens, set forth dimensions of the problem.

Institutions of higher education, he said, are responsible principally for issuing two types of records: a transcript which shows the complete and unabridged academic history of a student at that institution and a diploma which shows the degree awarded. In addition, institutions are required to complete numerous forms that contain information about attendance, enrollment, withdrawal, degrees, and related information.

The official transcript is "the single most important document or record issued by the institution. It contains both demographic and academic data. It shows in chronological order the complete history of [a student's] academic endeavors . . ." (U.S. Congress, House, 11 December 1985, pp. 80–88).

The issuance of transcripts is a high volume activity in most registrar offices. In a 1984 survey, eighty-eight institutions responded to an inquiry concerning the volume of transcript requests. These eighty-eight colleges and universities filled a total of 2,901,000 transcript requests for an average of 32,965 requests per institution per year. The smallest number of requests filled was 2,000; the largest, 390,000.

Both current and former students at American colleges and universities make transcript requests to verify their academic records for potential employers, as well as other admissions officers. Requests are made in person, by mail, and over the telephone. However, since passage of the Buckley Amendment of the Family Rights and Privacy Act of 1974, most institutions refuse to honor transcript requests made over the telephone unless the document is going directly from the sending institution to the receiving institution in connection with application for admission. Most institutions also now require personal identification before issuing transcripts to students.

Historically, transcript information (courses, grades, hours of credit, degrees, etc.) was hand-posted and manually duplicated. Although fraud existed during the early years, the problems became more widespread with the advent of photo reproduction, and more recently, computers. Today, administrators and faculty find themselves taking time to scrutinize transcripts much more carefully, attempting to detect fraudulent entries, if not identifying entire transcripts as fraudulent.

The Buckley amendment opened academic records to millions of alumni, as well as to currently enrolled students. Whereas prior to Buckley, most institutions did not issue official transcripts directly to students, today a student or former student can receive a copy of his or her record simply by asking for one. Accordingly, most institutions now mark their transcripts "Issued to Student" which generally makes them unacceptable as official documents for admissions at other institutions of higher education, certification to state licensing boards and, it is hoped, employment purposes.

Generally, transcript users will only accept as official transcripts that contain these items: an embossed institutional seal; the registrar's signature; and the date of issuance. In addition, most—but not all—of these users will not accept for admission purposes a transcript that is delivered in person by the student. Rather, official transcripts are mailed in sealed envelopes directly to the requested transcript recipient.

Transcript problems occur when institutional seals and signature stamps are lost or stolen. Other problems occur when users, particularly potential employers, do not bother to verify the authenticity of records of which they are suspicious. For example, if a transcript does not appear to be genuine or if it has been hand-delivered, the recipient would be prudent to telephone or write the institution to seek verification.

Too often, the potential employer does not require an official transcript, but chooses to accept an undocumented resume proclaiming certain educational and/or professional experiences. Many resumes containing claimed academic achievements, including degrees, go unverified.

Transcript "Verification"

Running a transcript verification business is another activity spinning off diploma mill operations. How convenient it is to have all of one's college transcripts stored in one place so that they can, for a fee, be duplicated and sped off to a variety of educational institutions or potential employers. What these "services" do not mention is that most college and university registrars insist that complete transcripts be sent directly to them by individual institutions; it is seldom acceptable to have such sensitive information conveyed by commercial organizations. Actually most associations of professional schools perform centralized registration functions on behalf of member institutions.

Counseling Businesses

Counseling activities are also a lucrative sideline for diploma mill operators. If a client doesn't enroll in an organization in which the counselor has a financial interest, he or she can at least be advised (for a price) about comparable higher education credential opportunities. Generally the brochure describing such activities is heavy on language mentioning that one never need enter a classroom in order to earn the degree desired.

Career counseling, another diploma mill spin-off, apparently generates plenty of money for questionable counselors, and the next step for many is educational counseling, once it has been determined that one's career goals can only be realized through pursuit of a college degree. Of course, the royal road may involve enrollment in an institution in which the counselor has a financial interest. Brochures describing educational options following such counseling generally emphasize how easy, and how fast, one can acquire a college degree.

A number of extremely aggressive entrepreneurial groups currently engage in marketing activities aimed at counseling prospective students in nursing programs. The administration of Nursing Programs for Regents College Degrees of The University of the State of New York has identified organizations that offer at very high prices services that are provided without charge by Regents College Degrees. Such services are frequently offered by individuals whose educational credentials suggest that they are not qualified to counsel. Also, it is not always made clear to prospective students that the organizations involved do not in any way represent Regents College Degrees—though some of them use Regents College Degree materials without authorization (Lettus, Marianne, 1987).

An example may give a flavor of these practices in their misrepresentation of Regents College Degrees in Nursing. One organization suggests it is possible to finish a degree in six months without mentioning that such achievement is possible only if the student has substantial transfer credits. Nor is it ordinarily possible for a student to complete a degree entirely by examination as is suggested in the same promotional materials. "Training-experiences" cannot, as claimed, be converted to college credit. Students earning Regents College Degrees must document learning equivalent to that required in a campus-based degree program by passing comprehensive, highly integrated, multiple choice examinations.

Financial counseling may also be an avenue of opportunity for smooth operators. Obviously, the appearance of legitimacy would be important here. In 1985, ACE's Division of Policy Analysis and Research was astonished to receive an unsolicited "donation" (its first) of $1,000 from an organization claiming to be a center for dissemination of information about financing a college education. The check was returned when it was learned that the organization had no legal standing in the state in which it was located and that the street address given was actually that of the post office in a large western city. The mailing address was simply a postal box number. Why would any organization try to make such a "donation?" The probable answer: so that in materials promoting its services, it could claim it had ties to a well-known organization representing the higher education community.

Honorary Doctorates

The problem of honorary doctorates issued by diploma mills has two aspects. On one side, degrees may be purchased by anyone in much the same way that fraudulent "earned" degrees of comparable worth are acquired. On the other, diploma mills apparently give degrees (without cost) to very well-known people.

A diploma mill may initiate the award of an honorary degree to a prominent person because the payoff here is that this name may then be mentioned in the organization's catalog or promotional literature, perhaps with a photograph showing the honoree accepting the award. Several very prominent persons in nations outside the United States have accepted these honorary degrees, perhaps in ignorance of the institution's standing in its home country.

At one foreign diploma mill doing business in the United States, the applicant for an honorary doctorate must submit an application form and enclose a *curriculum vita* "for consideration." Consideration of another kind is explicit on the same application where applicants must indicate whether upon acceptance, they will make a "donation" of $500, $1,500, $2,500, or $5,000.

False Certification

A certificate is a document issued by a governmental or nongovernmental agency to signify that an individual has fulfilled predetermined requirements and may use a specified professional or occupational title. While a certificate is not a degree, it is a respected document that carries implicit standards of academic achievement. At least one diploma mill operating as late as 1987, apparently from England, engaged in the clearly illegal practice of issuing certificates for which no academic performance is required. Some sixteen such certificates are available, ranging from dental technician to gemologist.

In the United States, the field of nutrition is a notable example in which questionable "certification" is a major problem. Far too many "nutritional consultants" proudly display impressive certificates and seek to identify themselves as legitimate advisors on health care.

Like diplomas, certificates are subject to fraudulent reproduction. In the hands of a skilled calligrapher, names and other words on certificates can be changed. But a Washington-based professional association recently uncovered an even more innovative technique. Not having degrees and other skills that would qualify her for a certificate of clinical competence from the association one individual went so far as to legally change her name to the name appearing on a legitimate certificate she had somehow acquired. When discovered, the woman had been in practice using the authentic certificate belonging to another person whose name she had appropriated.

It is a short step from the phony diploma, certificate or transcript to the letters of recommendation issued by some diploma mill operators. Such glowing letters must be effective when signed by the institution's president and sent along to a prospective employer.

Ready-Made Papers

The "term paper mill," whether an off-shoot of a diploma mill or an independent business, has been around for as long as there have been papers to write as a way of demonstrating the quality of academic performance. Some such organizations even publish catalogs, though they are filled with disclaimers such as "for research purposes only."

Papers and dissertations may be purchased ready-made, or they may be tailored to fit particular situations by speedy writers. "Custom research" is possible; so is "assistance" with theses and dissertations. Statistics, legal data, marketing surveys, even annotated bibliographies, all for overnight delivery at an additional fee are offered in a catalog received by one of the authors in mid-1987. The catalog contains more than 15,000 paper titles ranging from AIDS research to zoology.

Advertisements, which have been known to appear in very respectable publications, may feature "Editorial Services" or "Research Assistance." But the name of the game is fraud by producing a paper or dissertation that is not written by the person in whose name it will be submitted.

Class Rings

Anyone in the market for a diploma may also be in the market for a class ring. Acting on that belief, Anthony Geruntino, James Caffey, and company enclosed a brochure from "Joel Jewelry" with diplomas issued by "American Western University," one of several ephemeral organizations that were the targets of the FBI's Dipscam sweep in 1985 (U.S. vs. Geruntino, et al., p. 2). Class rings were allegedly offered by some of those indicted in the more recent (1987) FBI sweep. In the diploma mill realm, tie-in business connections are not unusual.

Directories

Clearly, one of the very best tools serving the diploma mill industry is a misleading directory. A number of these have been published and from all appearances they seem to be moneymakers both for their owners and for the owners of colleges and universities of questionable merit for which listings appear. These directories list legitimate, accredited institutions alongside those that do not have such recognition.

The listing for Harvard University, for example, may share a page with "Humbug U" which may appear to have the same characteristics as Harvard, including accreditation. What is not mentioned is that the accreditation of Humbug is from an organization not recognized by COPA.

Alleged diploma mills may also be listed in the directory, but there will be no statement of criteria the directory publisher used in assigning these organizations to diploma mill status. The inclusion of such a section does much to lend an air of legitimacy to other diploma mills that are carefully listed in another section along with institutions accredited by COPA-recognized agencies. The directory owner's financial interest in one or more nonaccredited institutions that are highly recommended may not be disclosed. If public disclosure is eventually made (presumably under pressure), the full extent of such financial interest may not be revealed.

Misleading directories can have disastrous consequences for an unsophisticated audience who take their inferences seriously. Take the case reported by a Washington-based professional association of two school teachers in a small east coast town who sought Ph.D.s from a legal, but vacuous, diploma mill in a midwestern state after reading about this organization in a directory. There were no classes to attend, but papers were assigned and graded. At the end of the road was a dissertation. The women paid their fees and worked hard to complete their term paper assignments and "dissertations." When they received their diplomas, they were informed that their dissertations had been "placed on file" in the Library of Congress. There was one little hitch, however. The university did not have accreditation though it had been billed as having "candidate for accreditation" status with an organization not recognized by COPA. Such accreditation was supposed to be "forthcoming" at the time the work at the institution was started, though it had not been obtained when the teachers finally finished their work.

To put it mildly, the teachers were dismayed when they stated their problem and asked for advice from their professional association in Washington. The facts were stark. Neither the U.S. Office of Education nor COPA had ever heard of the "accrediting" entity involved. For that matter, they had not heard of the "university" either, although its legal existence was eventually confirmed by others. Their degrees, obtained from an organization having few or no educational resources, facilities, or qualified faculty, were worthless.

Here is a summary of characteristics drawn from directories of dubious merit.

1. On the cover may be a photograph of an impressive public building even though the occupants of the building may have nothing whatever to do with postsecondary education. This device is particularly effective in deceiving foreign nationals who are accustomed to thinking of postsecondary education as a national government responsibility although it is not in the United States.

2. Such terms as "authorized", "chartered," "approved," "certified," "licensed," "recognized," and especially "accredited" are not defined at all or are defined in terms that are misleading as to their actual meaning in a postsecondary education context.

3. "Subscribers" to the directory may be listed in a manner that implies endorsement though such a list may be no more than institutions or organizations where an employee has purchased the directory in the past.

4. The owner of a directory may pose as a public guardian against diploma mills, while aiding, abetting, or perhaps being a business partner in such organizations.

5. Respectability by association may be sought by including in the directory the names of state officials, university faculty or administrators, or legitimate directories and guidebooks.

As can be seen, all manner of academic and legal documents and papers are subject to misuse or outright falsification. The full range of appurtenances that are fellow travelers with diploma mills is massive in scope. Any type of academic service can be misrepresented and corrupted.

14
Diplomas For Export: A Boom in Foreign Trade

The diploma mill problem often involves foreign nations, and as such is double-edged. First is the problem of American diploma mills operating overseas, and second, the problem of foreign diploma mills operating in the United States or awarding their degrees to American nationals overseas.

While statistics are elusive (not even the State Department has generated them), there is every indication that American diploma mills do a huge business overseas. Third World students are a prime market, but Europeans, too, are susceptible to the lure of easy American degrees, and some are snapping up degrees from highly questionable American institutions. In a 1986 article, the Italian journal *Il Mondo* asserted that Italian clients were motivated by the need "to satisfy the vanity, the amour-propre and the craving for a Doctor title. . . ." Typical degree-holders, the article claims, are "provincial industrialists (often no longer young), young managers, self-made men, sons of the rich not inclined to study" (Cometto, 1986).

In their heavy advertising and promotional campaigns, these institutions, mostly based in California, often list the names of individuals who have already acquired degrees. Some institutions have also enlisted the aid of prominent Italian television personalities.

In most nations of continental Europe, universities—including private universities—must be officially authorized by that government. Sometimes even a formal act of Parliament is required at either the national or provincial level. Institutions which do not have formal authorization usually find that their diplomas and degrees are not accepted.

However, beyond the central common bond of required governmental recognition, legal systems differ among nations with respect to authorizing educational institutions to exist or empowering them to confer degrees. In Austria and the Federal Republic of Germany, academic degrees are protected under the law. Foreign degrees may not be used, not even on business cards, unless they have been officially recognized by the national authorities.

In Switzerland and the United Kingdom, the laws are less stringent. Swiss private higher education institutions (including local branches of American-based private universities) do not need any formal authorization in most of the nation's cantons and may accordingly operate in full compliance with Swiss law. Still, their diplomas and degrees have no value in the eyes of Swiss authorities.

In the United Kingdom, the term "university" is not protected under the law, though a provision to limit the power to award degrees is pending in Parliament (United Kingdom, November 1987). Any private individual is free to open a university and offer degrees by correspondence. Although such correspondence institutions may have no Royal Charter, they are not illegal. In an amusing short story, novelist Graham Greene invents and spins a yarn about one of these, "St. Ambrose's, Oxford" (1973).

The story centers around Elisabeth Cross who goes to

work in the Oxford office of a diploma mill run by her uncle, a Mr. Nicholas Fennick. Mr. Fennick tells a friend he has in mind training Elisabeth "to act as bursar. The strain of being both bursar and president of the college is upsetting my stomach." But Elisabeth has her own reasons for joining the staff at St. Ambrose's. She wants a husband and figures going to work for a college at Oxford—even her uncle's carefully crafted diploma mill—is the way to do it. Elisabeth is quickly disillusioned. St. Ambrose's might boast "lots of picking for racketeers," but nothing that would help a girl catch a husband. At first, she sees the goings-on at St. Ambrose's pretty much as a joke, "but when she saw the money actually coming in, the whole thing seemed less amusing." She enters into the spirit of things and decides that the "suckers, when they took their diploma-degrees,would know several things they hadn't known before." Among the suckers, she eventually finds a husband, too. The son of a lord, sort of.

St. Ambrose's and its ilk aside, foreigners generally expect that almost any institution of higher education will have the full endorsement of either the state or federal governments of the United States. Knowing this, American diploma mill operators do all that is possible to foster the notion. An example from India will be sufficient to demonstrate this.

An American diplomatic office in India reports that it received in late 1986 a pathetic letter from an Indian citizen who had just received his Ph.D. by correspondence from an apparently illegal American diploma mill. It had all started with a newspaper advertisement run by an office in India associated with the institution.

The university certainly sounded respectable. Was it not listed alongside other well-known American universities in pages of various directories that had been sent on request? It even had an "affiliation" with one of these. There were a large number of impressive sounding names and titles of individuals on the letterhead. The university was "recognized" by the American government and also by the government of India. As if that were not enough, it was said to be "100 years old and owned by the government of the USA."

Payment of a stiff initial fee was followed by a request

that various study assignments be completed. Within several months, the enrollee was successfully convinced to send in more money in return for which he was issued something called a "coaching completion certificate."

Next came a request for even more money payable as an "exemption fee." The purpose of this was not entirely clear, although it was clear that the terminal degree in psychiatry would not be issued until the fee was paid. The client protested the amount and also the fact that no notice of this fee was given in prior materials that had been sent to him. This petition was successful. The fee was lowered and the degree issued. The entire process took place over a period of about six months.

Ultimately, the more credentialed, but poorer, individual found himself in possession of a degree that was worthless to qualify him to practice as a psychiatrist in India. Who can blame him for asking the American diplomats to "show me the right path for justice"?

Organizations based in California cause the most difficulty for honest, unwary consumers overseas—though the confusion can be played out to the benefit of unscrupulous individuals, too. As in the United States, the trouble arises because the terms "authorized," "approved," and "accredited" in the context of regulation by the California state government are not clearly explained or understood in foreign nations.

As previously noted, the California Private Postsecondary Education Division does not attempt to control the activities of California-based institutions in foreign countries. Consequently, such institutions are free to do almost anything outside of the state without damaging their standing with state government. Some organizations have developed very large overseas programs, directly stating or implying that their programs enjoy state authorization and/or approval. Indeed that may be true. What is not mentioned is that the state has not assumed any responsibility whatsoever for programs conducted by its authorized or approved institutions outside its borders.

While working as a consultant on the subject of accreditation in Saudi Arabia and some of the Persian Gulf states in 1987, Dr. Barbara Uehling, now Chancellor of the University of California at Santa Barbara, found herself besieged with questions about American diploma mills. She reports that a number of relatively sophisticated persons worked hard and paid as much as $6,000 before earning Ph.D. degrees from legal, but unaccredited, California institutions.

In a 1987 letter to ACE, a staff member at the U.S. Embassy in Saudi Arabia indicated the unwitting pursuit of a diploma mill degree has become "a real pitfall for ambitious Third World youth looking for a chance to better themselves." He reports many such individuals have paid "great sums of money for worthless degrees." Some have been deceived by advertisements placed by diploma mills in a local English language newspaper. The institutions are assumed to be legitimate when such a prominent newspaper carries the ad. Result: "U.S. education in general gets a black eye," according to the Embassy official (Miller, 19 April 1987). Of course, many foreigners obtaining diploma mill degrees are fully aware of the deceit that is implicit in the transaction.

The Council of Europe, an organization of twenty-one democratic European nations based at Strasbourg in France, has taken the lead in monitoring and attempting to control diploma mill activities. The Council has spelled out its definition of the term "recognition" as it applies to academic degrees. Recognition for academic purposes means that the degree is acceptable for securing admission to university studies or to teaching or research work in a reputable institution of higher education. Recognition for professional or vocational purposes means that the degree holder may qualify under a nation's laws to enter a particular profession or trade. Recognition may also refer to acceptance on the labor market where government regulations do not apply. Private employers in Europe, as a general rule, are free to accept any foreign degree as valid.

In 1972, the Council of Europe first published a list of what it termed "degree mills." More recently, it attempted to refine and widen this list in order to put the brakes on what it perceives as rampant diploma mill activity—mostly by organizations based in the United States. Because of various hazards and complications, the Council has called off its plan for publishing a list of "institutions whose degrees are not in general officially recognized in Europe." Instead, the list will be restricted to "internal government use only." The Council will, however, publish a "positive list . . . enumerating only recognized European universities," according to Michael Vorbeck, Head for the Section for Educational Research and Documentation, at the Council's offices in Strasbourg, France (1987).

Foreign countries also have their share of home-based diploma mills, some of which welcome business from American citizens. A few such organizations actually solicit business in the United States though there is no evidence that this practice equals the American-based traffic in the other direction.

An apparent proliferation of diploma mills in the United Kingdom has been acknowledged of late by none other than His Royal Highness, the Prince of Wales. Speaking at the fifth degree conferment ceremony of the Council of National Academic Awards, Prince Charles cited statistics showing that the nation's Department of Education had estimated the number of such organizations to have more than doubled in a two-year period. He also noted that "One or two actually have courses and examinations and distribute grand prospectuses describing their buildings. But in case you are thinking of visiting them, they actually add in capital letters: A previous appointment is necessary and a minimum of forty-eight hours notice must be given" (Jones, 1985, p. 58).

His Royal Highness may be especially sensitive. A European cousin of the diploma mill is the firm selling or awarding royal titles to anyone who will pay enough.

In addition to the United States, one other notable western hemisphere exporter of spurious diplomas is Colombia. According to a report from that nation's Ministry of Higher Education, fifty-six "fake universities" have been set up, including twenty-seven in the capital city of Bogotá. Costs may run as high as $650 each semester. In its August 14, 1985 issue, *The Chronicle of Higher Education* reported that a source in the Colombian Ministry of Education said that some of the institutions had "bought protection" by paying bribes to government inspectors. None of the degrees issued by these institutions is recognized by the Colombian Ministry of Higher Education.

Also reported in the *Chronicle* was the unorthodox practice of Rajasthan College in Jaipur, India of selling medical degrees for as much as $625 each. The College was also reported to have sold "phony degrees from colleges in other states" (Bhargava, 1987).

In sum, it is certainly true that American diploma mills are building a thriving industry based on the award of easy degrees to foreigners. So far, neither the federal nor state governments seem able to control the resulting problems. Nor have American higher education associations or accrediting agencies been able to exert a very assertive influence. This is unfortunate. Only diploma mills and their nefarious clients benefit from the present state of inaction and misunderstanding.

15
Conclusions: What Must Be Done to Make Things Better?

While the scope and intensity of the diploma mill problem in America has been aggravating, the problem itself is not a new one. For as long as there have been academic degrees in America there have been those who have sought to counterfeit or cheapen them. Printed materials giving evidence of diploma mill activities in the United States go back for more than one hundred years. Annual reports of the United States Commission on Education cite the problem, as do articles appearing in various journals (Association for Continuing Higher Education, September 1977, p. 10).

John Eaton, U.S. Commissioner of Education in 1876, expressed concern about fraudulent degrees being awarded not only to Americans but to foreign nationals who were already discovering the ease with which they could purchase American degrees. This announcement was seconded four years later when Andrew White, the American minister in Berlin, wrote his superior in the Department of State to complain about the threat that diploma mill activities posed to the integrity of legitimate American degrees.

In 1880, the *Philadelphia Record* reported that phony medical degrees were being sold for $445—a princely sum in those days (Bender and Davis, 1972). Headlines in the *Chicago Tribune* for December 8, 1872, highlighted "diplomas for cash" that were available from a Professor R. A. Van Angelbeeks. For just $30, "a man can get almost anything he wants," according to the article.

In September 1977, a special committee on quality in education of the Association for Continuing Higher Education (ACHE) issued a position paper on "Degree Granting Abuses." The committee was chaired by Lee Porter of Roosevelt University who in 1972 had written *Degrees for Sale,* an exposé of the problem. The Committee noted the scope and complexity of the diploma mill phenomenon giving particular attention to those portions of it that bore on development of nontraditional higher education.

Beginning in 1984, the U.S. House of Representatives' Subcommittee on Health and Long-Term Care of the Select Committee on Aging conducted an investigation of fraudulent medical degrees. Under direction of its Chairman, Rep. Claude Pepper (D-Florida), the Subcommittee concluded that diploma fraud constitutes a serious threat to the health and well-being of Americans.

The Pepper Subcommittee was not, however, the first agency of Congress to investigate the diploma mill problem. In 1924, a subcommittee of the Senate Committee on Education and Labor held hearings on degree-granting abuses. It recommended that evidence of diploma mills be collected and put on record, that governmental agencies cooperate in a single corrective effort, and that states enact stronger laws governing the operation of educational organizations (Reid, 1966,

p. 96). Unfortunately, progress toward any of these objectives has been slow or nonexistent.

The diploma mill problem is a continuing concern of ACE, a nonprofit education association representing accredited postsecondary institutions as well as national and regional higher education associations. In June 1958, the Council's Commission on Education and International Affairs studied the problem and offered possible solutions. This action was taken after it was learned that large numbers of foreign nationals were receiving degrees from highly questionable organizations in the United States. A book, *Degree Mills in the United States* by Robert H. Reid, and several monographs were among the outcomes of this study.

Responding to numerous complaints, in 1982, ACE's Office on Educational Credit and Credentials (now The Center for Adult Learning and Educational Credentials) began collecting information about diploma mills. This information-gathering effort has made it possible to analyze the diploma mill problem, using a database that had been lacking until now.

As Americans seek to protect the integrity of degrees awarded by colleges and universities they should set aside at least three commonly held assumptions about diploma mill activity that are erroneous. These assumptions are: (1) diploma mill activity is not widespread; (2) most diploma mill activity is illegal; and (3) a diploma mill transaction is, essentially, a victimless crime.

The record shows that diploma mills operate throughout the United States. The magnets that attract individuals toward diploma mill degrees are embedded in an increasingly credential conscious society. Millions of Americans cannot obtain the jobs they want, earn a promotion, or even retain their jobs without obtaining additional academic credentials. Still others desire credentials to enhance their social status. As individuals strive to meet job requirements or improve self-esteem, some may turn to the quick and easy route of a diploma mill degree.

Graduates of diploma mills can be found in nearly every

profession and vocation. Thousands of government workers, military personnel, business and professional people, university faculty and administrators, school teachers and administrators, engineering and technical workers, and medical and counseling personnel hold degrees from diploma mills. When the foreign market is considered, American diploma mills qualify in every way as an export industry. Foreigners, sophisticated and otherwise, flock to pay for their precious American parchment.

Illegal diploma mills have captured the attention of the FBI and the U.S. Postal authorities, but most diploma mill activity is legal under state authorization and related laws that are too often less than stringent. As many have proved, it is very easy to set up a university and even an accrediting agency and to go into business without violating the laws of some states.

Perhaps the most erroneous of common assumptions about diploma mills is that the typical mill transaction is essentially a victimless crime. Who gets hurt really when one crook buys a diploma from another, and both parties to the transaction are satisfied? While many unscrupulous individuals are well aware that they are, in effect, purchasing a degree, other unsophisticated people believe themselves to be dealing with a legitimate college or university. Many such individuals are foreigners who are unaware of the American system of accreditation as an instrument of academic quality assurance.

There are also indirect victims of diploma mill operators. Employers, including colleges and universities, who believe that applicants for employment or employees seeking promotion are presenting valid credentials are indirect victims. So are those who receive services (marriage or personal counseling, psychotherapy, medical treatment, etc.) from diploma mill graduates who do not, in fact, have the knowledge or skills that their credentials indicate. Foreigners who have earned degrees from fully accredited American colleges and universities may suffer if their credentials are undifferentiated from those awarded by questionable American organizations to fellow citizens.

But a chief indirect victim of diploma mill activity may

be legitimate and academically respectable nontraditional education. To the extent the concepts and tools of nontraditional education (e.g., external degrees, learning contracts, and especially assessment of prior college-level learning) are abused by diploma mill operators, the cutting edge of innovative and farsighted new programs will be damaged.

In 1977, the special committee on quality in education of the Association for Continuing Higher Education (Porter Committee) cited eight obstacles impeding progress in combating the diploma mill problem: (1) lax state laws; (2) few complaints from buyers and consumers; (3) the ability of diploma mill operators to move from state to state; (4) the profitable market for diploma mill degrees; (5) "too flexible" laws regarding tolerance for practitioners in various career fields; (6) American society's "fixation" on academic degrees; (7) insufficient awareness of the problem among influential persons in accrediting agencies, state education departments, and recognized universities; and (8) the profitability of diploma mill advertisements for for the publications that carry them (Association for Continuing Higher Education, September 1977, pp. 23–26). Most of these obstacles still apply today, although there have been some shifts in the degree of relative importance among them.

The laws in some states are still lax, though action has been taken in some states, notably in Arizona and California, to make it more difficult for individuals and groups to start organizations that may then be called colleges or universities. Diploma mill operators still move from state to state, always seeking the loose law or the lax enforcer. Also, state laws regulating occupational licensing are too weak in some instances.

Still driving the diploma mill machine is the American preoccupation with credentialing. To be blunt, it is often impossible to obtain many jobs or to qualify for advancement unless one has at least a baccalaureate and often a master's degree or a doctorate. For as long as diplomas represent value, they will be subject to counterfeiting in one form or another.

In his 1964 study of American degree mills, Robert Reid

took note of an absence of any sense of urgency among educators and the public about the problem of degree mills. Many persons had "the impression that there are still relatively few cases [of degree mill activity] and that these represent isolated instances; that most of these offenders were put out of business ages ago; that almost all such abuses exist in the fringe areas of the healing and spiritual arts and rarely in the respected professional fields; that people, especially foreigners, should 'know better'; that only fools and fakers get involved; that, after all, it doesn't really hurt anyone, is not a serious problem, and will eventually go away if you do not notice it" (Reid, 1966, pp. 245–246).

The Porter Committee also counted public apathy as a major hurdle to overcome in controlling diploma mills. Altogether too much disinterest still prevails among the educators of today—though a growing number of them are beginning to sit up and take notice as holders of degrees from diploma mills and marginal institutions take their places in industry, government, the military, and even, perhaps especially, in educational institutions. One incoming chief academic officer at an accredited university in the East was astonished to learn that two members of his faculty held diploma mill Ph.Ds. Reviews of diploma mill promotional pieces and catalogs reveal a surprising number of "successful alumni" holding responsible positions in respected professions, businesses, and institutions.

Publicity given the diploma mill problem in television shows such as "Today" and "60 Minutes" has roused the public to some extent. So did the hearings sponsored by the Pepper Subcommittee. Employers, too, are more aware than they once were that employees or potential employees might try to dupe them by presenting degrees that are not true degrees.

Diploma mills are still profitable, as Anthony Geruntino and others can attest. Diploma mill advertising still appears in too many respected publications.

What can be done to overcome these obstacles and make the nation a more honest place for individuals holding legitimate degrees and seeking opportunities to acquire degrees? No single solution or even array of solutions will completely correct the problem of diploma mill operation in America. These actions, however, are being recommended by The Center for Adult Learning and Educational Credentials of the American Council on Education.

1. *Develop, maintain, and publicize an information base or clearinghouse about institutions that do not have COPA-recognized accreditation or accreditation candidacy status.*

ACE now has at its Center for Adult Learning and Educational Credentials a data base of information about institutions and organizations that do not have accreditation or accreditation candidacy from an agency recognized by COPA. Not all such organizations, of course, are diploma mills, and it is not possible for the Center's staff to evaluate the educational quality of any such institution. ACE's objective in maintaining and using this base of information should be (and is) that of functioning as a clearinghouse for disseminating information within appropriate legal and ethical safeguards and guidelines.

2. *Urge the Education Commission of the States (ECS) to update and appropriately disseminate its "Model State Licensing Law," and recommend its adoption.*

In 1973, ECS developed a model licensing law that was used by a number of states in developing their own comparable legislation. ECS should update this document, retitle it "Model State Law for Authorizing Degree-Granting Postsecondary Education Institutions," and disseminate this information as appropriate to its members in each state.

3. *Encourage all states to review their laws pertaining to authorization or approval of educational institutions even in the absence of guidance from ECS, to strengthen them to at least the level suggested by the present version of the ECS model state licensing law, and to enforce them.*

The first bastion of defense against fraud and deception in higher education lies in state government. Enactment of new laws or amendment of old ones to deal directly with the problem should be a focus of attention in each state. Each state should evaluate its existing laws in relation to the model licensing law provided by ECS.

Sometimes a state may have adequate laws governing the organization and operation of degree-granting institutions but may not be enforcing them. In some instances this may be the result of staff shortages. In other instances, the demand for enforcement may be insufficient. Each appropriate agency of state government should feel pressure from citizens to enforce statutes already on the books.

4. *Urge state governments to adequately staff their regulatory offices—including the relevant enforcement agency (e.g., attorney general) as well as the agency charged with authorization of postsecondary education institutions.*

During the budgetary crunch of the past decade, a number of states have substantially reduced the number of staff employed in regulatory activities. No doubt some of these cutbacks were justified. However, it is shortsighted for a state to avoid its responsibilities for safeguarding the integrity of the postsecondary education institutions that it authorizes. The price paid for such an omission may be very high.

5. *Encourage national and regional associations of colleges and universities and faculty members and administrators to examine diploma mill practices as they affect their members and their work and careers respectively.*

Sessions at regional and national meetings of education associations should be part of such an effort. Appropriate actions by these bodies should be taken after specific problems have been identified.

6. *Encourage and facilitate federal government efforts to enforce federal laws regarding wire and mail fraud and unfair trade practices.*

The federal government should be encouraged (and helped) to enforce its laws governing fraudulent use of the U.S. mails and wire services. The U.S. Postal Inspection Service and the FBI are the agents of enforcement. With its ongoing Dipscam operation, the FBI (often in cooperation with the Postal Inspection Service) is performing well in this task. Both the

FBI and the Postal Inspection Service can use evidence of diploma mill activity (e.g., suspicious correspondence including the containing envelope) that may be supplied by individuals who receive it.

The Federal Trade Commission (FTC) should seek enforcement of federal laws prohibiting unfair and deceptive commercial practices (15 U.S. Code, Sections 41–58). At present, the FTC, as is its prerogative, assigns relatively low priority to diploma mills as targets for enforcement. This priority ranking should be changed to give the diploma mill problem a higher ranking.

7. *Urge the media not to accept advertising from extremely questionable institutions that claim to be colleges or universities.*

At present, the standards of many publications with respect to advertising are extremely casual. In 1979, after some members viewed a televised "60 Minutes" presentation on the diploma mill problem, the United States Association of Evening Students responded by adopting a resolution urging the President and Members of Congress "to make certain that all forms of home study and mail order higher education college degree programs are conducted in a legitimate manner." The organization also urged *The New York Times* (without success) to cease accepting ads for institutions the association considered might be diploma mills (Farma, 1979). (The *Times* has recently adopted a more responsible policy.)

8. *Urge employers to check the educational credentials claimed by employees or would-be employees with college and university officials.*

Employers are frequently lax about checking the credentials of persons applying for employment. This is curious in light of evidence showing that many resumes submitted by applicants contain false or at least misleading information. More sophisticated checking of educational credentials can help employers avoid mistakes in hiring and promoting employees.

9. *Urge victims (individuals or employers) to report di-*

ploma mill fraud to appropriate state and federal agencies (e.g., state government regulatory bodies, U.S. Postal Inspection Service, FBI, FTC).

Persons believing themselves to be victims of diploma mill operators can obtain help in many instances. Ordinarily the first avenue of complaint should be state government. (Appendix D is a listing of state agency personnel with brief summaries of relevant state statutes.)

Complaints about suspected mail fraud may be submitted to the U.S. Postal Inspection Service national or regional offices. Complaints about either mail fraud or wire fraud may be submitted to the national or regional offices of the FBI.

10. *Establish a base for national action aimed at continuous monitoring of diploma mill operations and development of corrective action.*

With its resource of information about diploma mills, ACE's Center for Adult Learning and Educational Credentials stands ready to function as a base for development and coordination of corrective action on the part of the higher education community. Many other institutions and agencies, however, must also mobilize to provide information and support.

Suppose someone suspects that a person claiming a degree has demonstrated something less than postsecondary-level learning? What can be done? The following actions may, in such instances, be helpful.

1. Obtain a current edition of *Accredited Institutions of Postsecondary Education* which is published annually for COPA by ACE (see Appendix C). Is the institution listed as accredited or in candidacy status with a COPA-recognized accrediting agency? If a college or university is not listed in this directory, can it be assumed that it is a diploma mill? Not necessarily. The point to keep in mind is that COPA recognition is a positive sign in the evaluation of the academic quality of a college or university. If an institution does not

have such recognition, it would be well to examine more closely the accreditation status that it claims, if any.

2. Write or call the person responsible for oversight of private postsecondary education institutions in the state of domicile for the institution in question (see Appendix D). Ask if the institution is currently authorized by the state to award degrees. If the institution is authorized but does not have COPA-recognized accreditation, ask the state government official what has been required by state government for the institution to hold the status it has with the state.

3. Obtain a copy of the institution's catalog. Examine it for evidence of diploma mill values as portrayed in the list of characteristics in chapter 3.

4. Ask for a copy of the person's Ph.D. dissertation or master's degree thesis. Dissertations or theses are often the best clue for anyone sniffing out a diploma mill. Many are simply descriptive, without comprehensive analysis. Others may give the appearance of quality but upon examination will be filled with content or methodological errors. Syntax, spelling, and organization may be seriously deficient. Ask the person pointed questions about the content of the dissertation; it may have been purchased ready-made. Some diploma mill Ph.D. degree holders will have no dissertation at all.

5. In the case of a claimed graduate degree, ask for the name of the person's major professor. A faculty member at an eastern university holding such a degree turned on his heel and walked out when challenged with just this question by a newly arrived chief academic officer. The faculty member was subsequently dismissed.

As is all too evident, the problem of diploma mills requires a public that is more well informed and alert about how such organizations operate. Group action by higher education associations, individual colleges and universities, and employers is required. The problem is complicated and more pervasive in American society than most members of the higher education community will admit. It is a problem that will not abate without informed and sustained corrective action.

Will a comprehensive attack on the problem of diploma mills in America be difficult? Yes it will, and victory will never be complete. But the stakes are high. What is at issue is nothing less than the integrity of degrees awarded by the nation's institutions of higher education. This is a battle that Americans cannot afford to lose.

Appendix A
Glossary of Acronyms

Acronym	Full Name
ACC	Association of American Colleges
AACJC	American Association of Community and Junior Colleges
AACRAO	American Association of Collegiate Registrars and Admissions Officers
AARTS	Association of Advanced Rabbinical and Talmudic Schools
ACE	American Council on Education
ACHE	Association for Continuing Higher Education
ACT PEP	American College Testing Proficiency Examination Program
AICS	Association of Independent Colleges and Schools
ASHA	American Speech–Language–Hearing Association
ASPA	American Society for Personnel Administration
ASTD	American Society for Training and Development
CAEL	Council for Adult and Experiential Learning
CETEC	Central University for Technical Studies [English translation]
CGS	Council of Graduate Schools in the United States
CIFIS	Central University for Social Investigation [English translation]
CLEP	College-Level Examination Program
CLEAR	Clearinghouse on Licensure, Enforcement and Regulation
COPA	Council on Postsecondary Accreditation
DANTES	Defense Activity for Non-Traditional Education Support
ECS	Education Commission of the States
FBI	Federal Bureau of Investigation
FTC	Federal Trade Commission
GAO	General Accounting Office

GED	General Educational Development [test]
NASA	National Aeronautics and Space Administration
NATTS	National Association of Trade and Technical Schools
NCAHF	The National Council Against Health Fraud, Inc.
NCATE	National Council for Accreditation of Teacher Education
NDIS	National Disciplinary Information System
NHSC	National Home Study Council
SACS	Southern Association of Colleges and Schools
3IC	Three-Institutional-Certification [method]
WASC	Western Association of Schools and Colleges

Appendix B

Important Addresses

American Association of
   Collegiate Registrars and
   Admissions Officers
   (AACRAO)
One Dupont Circle,
   Suite 330
Washington, D.C. 20036

American Association of
   Community and Junior
   Colleges (AACJC)
One Dupont Circle,
   Suite 410
Washington, D.C. 20036

American College
   Testing Proficiency
   Examination Program
ACT PEP Operations
The American College Testing
   Program
2201 North Dodge Street
Iowa City, IA 52243

American Council on
   Education (ACE)
The Center for Adult Learning
   and Educational
   Credentials
One Dupont Circle,
   Suite 1B-20
Washington, D.C. 20036

Association of American
   Colleges (AAC)
1818 R Street, NW
Washington, D.C. 20009

The College Board
45 Columbus Avenue
New York, NY 10023-6917

Council for Adult and
   Experiential Learning
   (CAEL)
10840 Little Patuxent Parkway
Columbia, MD 21044

Council of Europe
Section for Educational
   Research and
   Documentation
Secretariat General
BP 431 R6
67006 Strasbourg Cedex
Strasbourg, France

Council of Graduate Schools in
   the United States (CGS)
One Dupont Circle, Suite 430
Washington, D.C. 20036-1173

Council on Postsecondary
   Accreditation (COPA)
One Dupont Circle, Suite 305
Washington, D.C. 20036

Education Commission of the States (ECS)
1860 Lincoln Street, Suite 300
Denver, CO 80295-0301

Federal Bureau of Investigation (FBI)
6010 Kenley Lane
Charlotte, NC 28210
[Inquiries or information may also be referred to other regional offices of the FBI.]

Federal Trade Commission (FTC)
Division of Advertising Practices
Washington, D.C. 20580

The National Council Against Health Fraud, Inc. (NCAHF)
Trinity Lutheran Hospital
3030 Baltimore
Kansas City, MO 64108
Telephone: 800-821-6671

State Higher Education Executive Officers Association (SHEEO)
1860 Lincoln Street, Suite 310
Denver, CO 80295

U.S. Department of Education
Agency Evaluation Staff
Higher Education Management Services
Office of Postsecondary Education
Washington, D.C. 20202
[Inquiries about recognition of accrediting agencies]

U.S. Department of Education
Higher Education Institutional Eligibility Branch
Division of Eligibility and Certification
Debt Collection and Management Assistance Service
Office of Postsecondary Education
Washington, D.C. 20202
[Inquiries about eligibility of degree-granting institutions]

U.S. Postal Inspection Service
Postal Inspector in Charge
P.O. Box 96096
Washington, D.C. 20066-6096
[Inquiries or information may also be referred to regional offices of the U.S. Postal Inspection Service.]

Appendix C
Bibliographic Resources

What follows is not an exhaustive listing of bibliographic resources. Rather, it is a listing of those resources cited, that were especially useful, or that seemed especially significant in preparing this study of diploma mills in the United States.

Publications or Papers

ACSH News and Views. "Meet Sassafras Herbert, Professional Nutritionist." September/October 1983, p. 3.

Allen, G. Jack, and Grover J. Andrews. "Final Report of the Case Study of Off-Campus Postsecondary Education on Military Bases." Council on Postsecondary Accreditation. Report prepared for the Office of the Secretary of Defense under Defense Activity for Non-traditional Education Support (DANTES), 1980.

American Association of Collegiate Registrars and Admissions Officers. "Directory of Colleges and Universities with Non-traditional Educational Programs/Systems/Practices." May 1987.

American Association of Collegiate Registrars and Admissions Officers. "Misrepresentation in the Marketplace: Recognizing Fraudulent Credentials." February 1987.

American Association of Community and Junior Colleges. "The Associate in Applied Science Degree," Policy Statement. April 1986.

American Association of Community and Junior Colleges. "The Associate Degree," Policy Statement. October 1984.

American Association of Community and Junior Colleges. "Resolution on Accreditation of Associate Degree Granting Institutions." April 1987.

American Council on Education. *Fact Book on Higher*

Education 1986–87. New York: American Council on Education/Macmillan, 1987.

American Council on Education. *The Guide to the Evaluation of Educational Experiences in the Armed Services*. New York: American Council on Education/Macmillan (published every two years).

American Council on Education, The Center for Adult Learning and Educational Credentials. "Model Policy on Awarding Credit for Extrainstitutional Learning." June 1987.

American Council on Education. *The National Guide to Educational Credit for Training Programs*. New York: American Council on Education/Macmillan (published annually).

American Council on Education. "Recommendations on Credentialing Educational Accomplishment." The Task Force on Educational Credit and Credentials, 1978.

American Council on Education, Council on Postsecondary Accreditation, and American Association of Collegiate Registrars and Admissions Officers. "Joint Statement on Transfer and Award of Academic Credit." Self-Regulation Initiatives: Guidelines for Colleges and Universities, No. 4. January 1980.

American Speech-Language-Hearing Association. *Asha*, June 1985, p. 5.

Association for Continuing Higher Education. "Degree Granting Abuses." Report of a special committee on quality in education (Lee Porter, Chairman), September 1977.

Association of American Colleges. "Integrity in the College Curriculum: A Report to the Academic Community." The findings and recommendations of the "Project on Redefining the Meaning and Purpose of Baccalaureate Degrees." 1985.

Bender, L.W., and J.A. Davis. "Danger: Will External Degrees Reincarnate Bogus Degree Mills?" *Center for State and Regional Leadership*, Florida State University, July 1972. (As noted in Association for Continuing Higher Education. "Degree Granting Abuses." Report of a special committee on quality in education, Lee Porter, Chairman, September 1977.)

Bhargava, Arati. "Indian Officials Struggle to Improve

Corruption-Ridden Universities." *The Chronicle of Higher Education*, 10 June 1987.

Brown, Jonathan. "Accreditation and Licensure—How Does the State Assure Itself of Quality Control in Higher Education?" Issue Paper No. 16, Association of Independent California Colleges and Universities, revised 25 June 1987.

California Postsecondary Education Commission. "Changes in California State Oversight of Private Postsecondary Education Institutions." Staff Report Series, Commission Report 87-16, March 1987.

California Postsecondary Education Commission. "Public Policy, Accreditation, and State Approval in California." Commission Report 84-28, Adopted 23 July 1984.

California Postsecondary Education Commission, Special Committee for the Review of Out-of-State Accredited Institutions. "Oversight of Out-of-State Accredited Institutions Operating in California. A Report to the California Postsecondary Education Commission Pursuant to Senate Bill 1036." Report 85-35, March 1986.

California State Department of Education. "California Degree-Granting Authority and Recognition." Private Postsecondary Education Informational Bulletin No. 31, April 1985.

California State Department of Education, Council for Private Postsecondary Educational Institutions. "Issue: Consumer Complaints: Summary/Analysis FY 1984-85" (undated).

California State Department of Education, Council for Private Postsecondary Educational Institutions. "Protocol." Adopted January 1977 (Revised September 1983).

California State Department of Education, The Council for Private Postsecondary Educational Institutions. OPPE Information Bulletin Number 26, June 1983.

California State Department of Education, Division of Adult and Community Education, Office of Private Postsecondary Education. "Superintendent's Regulations, California Administrative Code, Title 5, Division 21 to Implement the Private Postsecondary Education Act of 1977." Effective April 1979.

California State Department of Education, Office on Private Postsecondary Education. "Enrollment Agreements, Contracts, and Other Instruments Evidencing Indebtedness." OPPE Information Bulletin No. 2, January 1978 (revised February 1979).

California State Department of Education, Private Postsecondary Education Division. "California Private Degree-Granting Institutions 'Approved' or 'Authorized' by the California Superintendent of Public Instruction." Effective 1 January 1986.

California State Department of Education, Private Postsecondary Education Division. "The Formally Adopted Developmental Guidelines for Reviewing Degree-Granting Institutions Pursuant to California Education Code Section 94310(c)." March 1985.

California State Department of Education, Private Postsecondary Education Division. "Guidelines for the Approval of Degree Granting Institutions Pursuant to California Education Code Section 94310 (b)." March 1986.

California State Department of Education, Private Postsecondary Education Division. "Guidelines for the Approval of Degree Granting Institutions and Programs Pursuant to California Education Code Section 94310 (b)." September 1985.

California State Department of Education, Private Postsecondary Education Division. "Instructions and Information for the Authorization of a Degree-Granting Institution Pursuant to California Education Code Section 94310 (c)." February 1985.

California State Department of Education, Private Postsecondary Education Division. "Instructions and Information for the Authorization of Degree-Granting Schools of Theology Pursuant to California Education Code Section 94310 (d)." December 1984.

California State Department of Education, Private Postsecondary Education Division. "The Private Postsecondary Education Act of 1977, as Amended 1984 (Reprint of Chapter 3, Part 59, Division 10, California Education Code)." January 1985 Reprint.

California State Department of Education, Private Postsecondary Education Division. "The Private Postsecondary Education Act of 1977, as Amended 1986." (Reprint of Chapter 3, Part 59, Division 10, California Education Code), January 1987 Reprint.

California State Department of Education, Private Postsecondary Education Division. "Superintendent's Regulations, California Administrative Code, Title 5, Education, Division 21, Private Postsecondary Education Institution," (Includes Amendments through October 1985).

The Chronicle of Higher Education. "Dispatch Case." 14 August 1985.

The College Board. "Moving Ahead with CLEP," 1986.

The College Board. *Overseas Educational Advisers Manual,* 1987.

Cometto, Maria Teresa. "Degrees for Sale: Step Right in Doctor!" *Il Mondo,* 11 August 1986. (English translation supplied by Council of Europe)

Council for Private Postsecondary Educational Institutions. "Annual Report to California Postsecondary Education Commission." Prepared in cooperation with Superintendent of Public Instruction, 1 July 1983–30 June 1984.

Council for Private Postsecondary Educational Institutions (California). "Standards for Authorization of Private Postsecondary Educational Institutions," 17 November 1982.

Council of Graduate Schools in the United States. "The Doctor of Philosophy Degree." A policy statement prepared by the Publications Committee, April 1982.

Council of Graduate Schools in the United States. "The Master's Degree." April 1981.

Council of Graduate Schools in the United States. "Non-Residential Graduate Degree Programs: A Policy Statement." June 1977.

Council on Postsecondary Accreditation. "The Balance Wheel of Accreditation." July 1987 (updated annually).

Council on Postsecondary Accreditation. "COPA Self-Study Advisory Panel: Findings and Recommendations." 2 October 1986.

Council on Postsecondary Accreditation. "Policy Statement on Off-Campus Credit Programs." 20 April 1983.

Council on Postsecondary Accreditation. "Provisions and Procedures for Becoming Recognized as an Accrediting Body for Postsecondary Educational Institutions or Programs." July 1987.

Education Commission of the States. "Model State Legislation." Report of the Task Force on Model State Legislation for Approval of Postsecondary Educational Institutions and Authorization to Grant Degrees. Report No. 39, June 1973.

18 U.S. Code, Sections 1341, 1342, 1343, and 1345.

Farma, Anthony F. Letter to President Jimmy Carter, 19 July 1979.

15 U.S. Code, Sections 41–58.

Fischer, Jack. "Counterfeit Diplomas Shatter System of Trust." *Dallas Times Herald*, 25 March 1985.

Gray, Thorne. "Willie Brown's Role Criticized in Grant to Eye Center." *Sacramento Bee*, 27 October 1985.

Greene, Graham. "When Greek Meets Greek" in *Collected Stories*. New York: Viking Press, 1973.

Gubser, Lyn, and Richard M. Millard. "Academic Fraud: A Threat To Quality." AASCU Studies 1982/1, American Association of State Colleges and Universities, April 1982.

Harris, John W., William E. Troutt, and Grover J. Andrews. "The American Doctorate in the Context of New Patterns in Higher Education." Council on Postsecondary Accreditation, 1980.

Harris, Sherry S. (ed.). *1986–87 Accredited Institutions of Postsecondary Education*. Published for the Council on Postsecondary Accreditation. Washington, D.C.: American Council on Education (published annually).

Herbert, Victor. "Legal Aspects of Specious Dietary Claims." *Bulletin of the New York Academy of Medicine*, Secondary Series, Vol. 58, No. 3, April 1982, pp. 242–253.

Herbert, Victor, William T. Jarvis, and Grace Powers Monaco. "Commentary: Obstacles to Nutrition Education." *Health Values: Achieving High Level Wellness*, 7 March/April 1983, pp. 38–41.

Hexter, Holly, and Charles J. Andersen. "Admission and Credit Policies for Adult Learners." Higher Education Panel Report No. 72, American Council on Education, December 1986.

Jarvis, William T. "Consumer Protection: An Educator's Viewpoint," *Association of Food and Drug Officials Quarterly Bulletin*, 50, January 1986, pp. 24–32.

Jones, Lyndon. Quote from Charles, Prince of Wales. "Diploma Mills—Part I: Origin and Growth." *Education and Training*, February 1985, p. 58.

Lenn, Marjorie Peace. "Accreditation, Certification, and Licensure," in M.A.F. Rehnke (ed), *Creating Career Programs in a Liberal Arts Context*. New Directions for Higher Education, No. 47, San Francisco: Jossey-Bass, 1987, pp. 49–63.

Lettus, Marianne K. Letters to David W. Stewart, 6 and 12 May 1987.

Ludlow, Nancy S. Interview with Michael P. Lambert in *The American Journal of Distance Education*, 1:2, 1987, pp. 67–71.

Malizio, Andrew G., and Douglas R. Whitney. "Educational Credentials in Employment: A Nationwide Survey." Research Brief, American Council on Education, Office on Educational Credit and Credentials, May 1985. (Revision of paper presented at 1984 American Association of Adult and Continuing Education Conference, Louisville, Kentucky, 9 November 1984.)

McGrath, Ellie. "Sending Degrees to the Dogs." *Time*, 2 April 1984, p. 90.

McQuaid, E. Patrick. "My Ph.D. Came Postage Due." *Science*, April 1985, pp. 51–56.

Meyers, Laura. "Stepping on the Quacks." *Health*, February 1984, pp. 115–117.

Miller, Ellsworth. Letter to David W. Stewart, 19 April 1987.

Minnesota Higher Education Coordinating Board. "Associate Degree Standards." Report of the Task Force on Associate Degree Standards, March 1986.

New England Association of Schools and Colleges, Inc., Commission on Institutions of Higher Education. *Accreditation Handbook*, 1983 Edition.

Pence, Robert L., Special Agent in Charge, and Raymond J. Bowley, Supervisory Special Agent, Federal Bureau of Investigation, U.S. Department of Justice, Charlotte, NC.

(Date of Search Warrant: 14 June 1984. Form letter undated but information supplemented and confirmed in telephone conversations with Otho Allen Ezell and Robert L. Pence.)

Porter, Lee. *Degrees for Sale*. New York: Arco, 1972.

Reid, Robert H. *Degree Mills in the United States*. Authorized reprint of original edition, produced by Microfilm-Xerography by University Microfilms, Inc., Ann Arbor, MI, 1966 (Based on dissertation written in 1963, Copyrighted 1964).

Satchell, Michael. "How I Bought My Degree." *Parade Magazine*, 8 January 1984, pp. 16–17.

Seper, Jerry, and Richard R. Robertson. "Diploma Mills: the Paper Merchants." *The Arizona Republic*, 6,7,8,9 March 1983.

Skinner, Patricia. Letter to David W. Stewart, 21 May 1987.

Skinner, Patricia. "Ohio Recognizes Critical Components for Quality Off-Campus Programs." *The Journal of Continuing Higher Education*, Winter 1987a, pp. 20–23.

Spille, Henry A., and David W. Stewart. "The New Breed of Diploma Mills: Numerous, Tough, and Aggressive." *Educational Record*, Spring 1985, pp. 16–22.

Staats, Craig. "Even a Dog Can Be a Nutrition Consultant." *Oakland Tribune*, Oakland, CA, 15 August 1983.

The State University of New York, "College Credit Recommendations: The Directory of the National Program on Noncollegiate Sponsored Instruction." The State Education Department, 1985–86.

Stewart, David W. "Protecting the Integrity of Academic Degrees." A report to the Commission on Educational Credit and Credentials. American Council on Education, September 1982.

Sullivan, Eugene (ed.). *Guide to External Degree Programs in the United States*, Second Edition. New York: American Council on Education/Macmillan, 1983.

34 U.S. Code, Sections 603.3 and 1141(a).

39 U.S. Code, Section 3005.

United Kingdom, Department of Education and Science. "A Provision To Limit the Power To Award UK Degrees." November 1987.

United States of America vs. Anthony James Geruntino, et al., Docket No. C-CR-85-22, United States District Court for the Western District of North Carolina, Charlotte Division, 6 February 1985.

United States of America vs. Frank George Pany, Docket No. C-CR-86-14, United States District Court for the Western District of North Carolina, Charlotte Division, 3 February 1986.

United States of America vs. Norman Bradley Fowler, et al., Docket No. C-CR86-100, United States District Court for the Western District of North Carolina, Charlotte Division, 3 December 1986.

U.S. Congress, House, "Fraudulent Credentials." Joint hearing before the Subcommittees on Health and Long-Term Care and Housing and Consumer Interests, Select Committee on Aging, 99th Congress, first session, Washington, DC, 11 December 1985 (Comm. Pub. 99-550).

U.S. Congress, House, "Fraudulent Credentials: Federal Employees." A report by the chairman of the Subcommittee on Health and Long-Term Care of the Select Committee on Aging, 99th Congress, second session, Washington, DC, April 1986 (Comm. Pub. No. 99-551).

U.S. Congress, House, "Fraudulent Credentials: Federal Employees." Hearing before the Subcommittee on Health and Long-Term Care, Select Committee on Aging, 99th Congress, second session, Washington, DC, 18 April 1986 (Comm. Pub. No. 99-571).

U.S. Congress, House, "Fraudulent Medical Degrees." Hearing before the Subcommittee on Health and Long-Term Care, Select Committee on Aging, 98th Congress, second session, Washington, DC, 7 December 1984 (Comm. Pub. 98-495).

U.S. Department of Education, Office of Postsecondary Education, Higher Education Management Services. "Nationally Recognized Accrediting Agencies and Associations." October 1986.

U.S. Postal Inspection Service. *Law Enforcement Report.* Spring 1985, p. 19.

Vorbeck, Michael. Letter to David W. Stewart, 27 June 1987.

Walters, Dan. "Diploma Mills a Painful Subject." *Sacramento Bee,* 15 June 1987.

Western Association of Schools and Colleges, Accrediting Commission for Senior Colleges and Universities. *Handbook of Accreditation.* March 1982.

Whitney, Douglas R., and Andrew G. Malizio (eds.). *Guide to Educational Credit by Examination,* Second Edition. New York: American Council on Education/Macmillan, 1987.

Willingham, Warren W. *Principles of Good Practice in Assessing Experiential Learning.* Columbia, MD.: Council for the Advancement of Experiential Learning, 1977.

Wittstruck, John R. "Requirements for Certificates, Diplomas and Associate Degrees: A Survey of the States." Denver, CO: State Higher Education Executive Officers Association, April 1985.

Wittstruck, John R. "State Oversight of Degree Granting Authority in Proprietary Institutions: Report of a SHEEO Survey." Denver, CO: State Higher Education Executive Officers Association, January 1984.

Young, Kenneth E., Charles M. Chambers, H.R. Kells, and Associates. *Understanding Accreditation.* San Francisco: Jossey-Bass, 1983.

Interviews

Interviews or, more often, informal telephone conversations from which cited materials were drawn were conducted with the following persons: Ellen Benkin, University of California, Los Angeles (11 May 1987); Otho Allen Ezell, FBI (1983–1987); Clara H. Lawhead, Pasco County (Florida) Health Department (1987–1988); E. Patrick McQuaid, Education Commission of the States (25 August 1987); Robert L. Pence, FBI (1984); Peter Reinecke, U.S. Congressional staff (1987); Barbara Uehling, University of California at Santa Barbara (1987); and Michael Vorbeck, Council of Europe (1985–1987). In addition, several telephone conversations were held with an inmate at a federal correctional facility who wishes to remain anonymous (1987).

Appendix D
Summary of State Statutes Governing State-Authorized Institutions Awarding Degrees at the Postsecondary Level with Names and Addresses of Persons Providing State Oversight

The one-paragraph summaries that follow have been developed from results of an ACE survey sent to persons responsible for overseeing nonpublic, degree-granting institutions in each state, except Hawaii which does not respond to such surveys. A reply to the survey was received from all states, as well as from the District of Columbia and Puerto Rico. The statutes in each state have been categorized as (1) relatively strong, (2) average strength, or (3) relatively weak.

In making these determinations, the following general criteria were used in labeling statutes as "relatively strong:"

1. Preoperation review with minimum criteria for authorized operation specified
2. Site visit required
3. Few or no exemptions from regulation except for in-

stitutions having accreditation from an agency recognized by COPA or recognized by the U.S. Department of Education
4. Finances reviewed for adequacy including attention to audits and insurance
5. Periodic "reauthorization" required
6. Activities of recruiting agents regulated
7. List of institutions authorized to operate maintained
8. Restrictions apply against misleading advertising
9. Out-of-state institutions regulated in manner comparable to those domiciled in the state (or reciprocity arrangements with strong statute states)
10. Penalties listed for violators of statutes.

Statutes are declared to be "relatively weak" if they do not contain provisions of the kind specified in the foregoing paragraph. Statutes labeled as of "average strength" tend to fall somewhere between "strong" and "weak" as described by these criteria.

All of the officials responding to the survey were given an opportunity to react to proposed summaries of their statutes and to the categorization of such statutes as "relatively strong," "average strength," or "relatively weak." Requests for change in any of the narratives were carefully considered. However, the final determination as to the wording of each summary and its categorization was made by the authors of this volume. These categorizations are *not* a commentary on the intensity or quality of oversight and enforcement activities by the designated state agencies. They do represent judgments as to the relative strength of state statutes.

Several words of caution are in order about interpretation of these summaries. The relative strength of a state's statutes is not the only factor affecting control of questionable institutions operating within a state's boundaries. Strong statutes may not be adequately enforced. Relatively weak statutes, if aggressively enforced, may be a deterrent to diploma mill activity. State administrative regulations and codes that implement statutes may also be important and have been taken into account in the summaries for some states.

Following each summary paragraph are names and addresses of those people responsible for oversight activities of nonpublic, degree-granting institutions in each state. Also listed are contact persons (designated "C") in some states at agencies having no explicitly specified oversight activities; these persons are listed because the state wishes to keep abreast of activities in this area. For an analysis of state statutes and enforcement efforts, readers are referred to chapter 10, "State Laws: The Baseline Defenses" and chapter 11, "California: A Very Special Case."

Alabama

A site visit with preoperation review is required for authorization. A $10,000 surety bond is also required. Recruiting agents are regulated and must be bonded and licensed. There are restrictions against misleading advertising. A relatively large number of categories of institutions are exempt from the statutes, for example, "schools operated on a nonprofit basis and offering only courses or programs of study in the performance of or preparation for the ministry of any established church, denomination, or religion." The Alabama State Department of Education may institute such actions as may be necessary to enforce the statutes. In addition to any other remedy, the Department may apply for relief by injunction, mandamus, or any other appropriate remedy in equity without being compelled to allege or prove that an adequate remedy at law does not otherwise exist. Violations of the statute are considered as misdemeanors and are punishable upon conviction by a fine of not more than $500 or imprisonment for a term of not more than six months, or both. (Average Strength Statutes)

Charles Saunders
Coordinator of Private Schools Unit
Department of Education
Room 348
State Office Building
Montgomery, AL 36130
(205) 261-2910

Alaska

A site visit for both initial and renewal authorization is required for all in-state institutions, but not for out-of-state institutions applying for authorization. Review includes attention to finances as well as program quality. Authorization is usually granted for one or two years initially and for two or three years thereafter. Surety bonds (institutional and for agents) are required in an amount proportional to the tuition income of the institution. The Commission on Postsecondary Education has the authority to grant exemptions to nonprofit postsecondary education institutions offering courses (except by correspondence) acceptable for credit toward associate, bachelor's or graduate degrees. Penalties apply for violations of the state statutes. (Average Strength Statutes)

Linda Low
Director for Institutional Authorization
Alaska Commission on Postsecondary Education
3601 C Street, Suite 478
Anchorage, AK 99503
(907) 561-4207

Arizona

A relatively new statute (January 1, 1985) was enacted to combat what had been a diploma mill epidemic. The statute requires that all degree programs be accredited by an accrediting agency recognized by the U.S. Department of Education or COPA. Institutions not yet accredited must post a $15,000 surety bond and are subject to a site visit to verify the institution's quality. Authorization is required for specific degree programs and for institutions. Agents of educational organizations are regulated. Restrictions are placed against misleading advertising, and civil/criminal penalties are listed for violations of the state statutes. (Relatively Strong Statutes)

Dona Marie Markley
Director, State Board for Private Postsecondary
   Education
1812 West Monroe
Room 214
Phoenix, AZ 85007
(602) 255-5709

Arkansas

Educational institutions in Arkansas must incorporate, and all institutions that wish certification (authorization) by the state must be accredited by an agency recognized by COPA. On-site visits are required. Authorization is accomplished in two stages. An institution authorized after review for the first stage may engage in planning and development only. Only after authorization at the second stage may degrees be awarded. Authorization is typically renewed every two years. A grandfather clause exempts from provisions of the statute religious institutions in operation prior to 1975. The State Department of Education requires surety bonding of agents. Violators of the statutes may be guilty of a misdemeanor and, if convicted, may be fined not more than $1,000 or be imprisoned not more than three months. (Relatively Strong Statutes)

John Spraggins (Dr.)
Associate Director for Academic Affairs
Arkansas Department of Higher Education
1220 West 3rd Street
Little Rock, AR 72201-1904
(501) 371-1441

Dorris R. Robinson-Gardner (Dr.)
Coordinator of Academic Programs
Department of Higher Education
1220 West 3rd Street
Little Rock, AR 72201-1904
(501) 371-1441

California

Until 1984, California's laws governing nonaccredited, degree-granting, private postsecondary education institutions were largely permissive in that they permitted the existence under an authorization statute of institutions that were virtually immune from state inspection and review. As a result, a large number of very questionable institutions received authorization and operated in apparent compliance with California's laws. Between 1978 and 1984 changes were made in that authorization statute, strengthening the state's authority—with the most recent amendments requiring an on-site review to verify that the authorized institution meets minimal state standards. In addition to authorization, the state has an "approval" status that is granted to institutions that the state determines meets established institutional standards. (This approval process is sometimes claimed as "equivalent to accreditation" which is not the case.) The California law also requires that institutions based outside of the state, seeking to operate within the state, undergo a separate state approval process. All institutions authorized or approved (including out-of-state approved) are required to undergo periodic state reauthorization or reapproval procedures. A number of authorized or approved institutions in California operate off-campus programs in other states and in foreign countries. The California Department of Education's Private Postsecondary Education Division does not review these programs in making its decisions with respect to authorization or approval. A special category of authorization applies to institutions awarding degrees in theology or religion. Certain other religious institutions are not covered by the state's Education Code. Under California's newly strengthened laws, many marginal institutions are being closed or are not choosing to reapply for authorization under the stricter requirements. (For more detailed information about the unique history of California's statutes and enforcement mechanisms, refer to chapter 11 of this volume.) (Average Strength Statutes)

Joseph P. Barankin (Dr.)
Assistant Superintendent of Public Instruction
    and Director
Private Postsecondary Education Division
California State Department of Education
721 Capitol Mall, P.O. Box 944272
Sacramento, CA 94244-2720
(916) 322-1852

Roy W. Steeves
Assistant Director
Private Postsecondary Education Division
California State Department of Education

601 West Fifth Street, Suite 910
Los Angeles, CA 90017
(213) 620-4256

Colorado

Nonaccredited, degree-granting institutions are required to make continual, reasonable, and timely progress toward accreditation by an agency recognized by COPA and to have an on-site (in Colorado) accreditation visit. Institutions are prohibited from advertising or initiating programs not first designated as holding potential to achieve accreditation by a COPA-approved accrediting association. Initial authorization status may then be granted by the Colorado Commission on Higher Education. Institutions are required to register annually with the Commission. No bonds are required, and no specific restrictions regarding misleading advertising exist under the higher education statutes. It is a misdemeanor under Colorado statutes to violate terms of the authorization laws. (Average Strength Statutes)

Timothy M. Grieder (Dr.)
Director, Continuing Education and Extended
  Academic Programs
Colorado Commission on Higher Education
1300 Broadway, 2nd Floor
Denver, CO 80203
(303) 866-2723

Connecticut

Any institution offering credits and degrees at the college level must be "licensed" and/or "accredited" by the Board of Governors for Higher Education. (Licensure in Connecticut means "approval to operate an institution or programs of higher learning at a specific location(s) for a specified period. Licensure does not provide authority to confer degrees." Accreditation as used by the Connecticut government means "approval . . . to operate an institution or program of higher learning at a specific location(s) for a specified period and to confer specified degrees. This type of accreditation should not be confused with COPA-recognized accreditation which is not a governmental function.) Connecticut explicitly requires on-site visits to educational institutions to verify the quality of the facilities and programs. Authorizations must be renewed every three years. State "accreditation" must be renewed every five years. Restrictions are in place against misleading advertisements by educational organizations. (Relatively Strong Statutes)

Donald H. Winandy (Dr.)
Director of Licensure and Accreditation
Board of Governors for Higher Education
61 Woodland Street
Hartford, CT 06105
(203) 566-2325

Delaware

The Department of Public Instruction is charged with recommending for authorization degree-granting programs in all nonpublic institutions. It has like responsibilities for authorization of all private and business trade schools. Evaluation of both programs and finances of these educational institutions is accomplished. Out-of-state institutions must also undergo review and approval under the same guidelines applying to in-state institutions. (Average Strength Statutes)

Ervin C. Marsh (Dr.)
State Supervisor, Certification and Personnel Division
Department of Public Instruction
Townsend Building, Box 1402
Dover, DE 19901
(302) 736-4688 or 736-4686

District of Columbia

Washington, D.C., requires a three-year provisional authorization and a site visit to educational institutions by the Educational Institute Licensure Commission and/or its designee. Washington requires authorization for each specific degree program. Site visits are required every five years for renewal of authorization if the institution is nonaccredited. Corporations may require their treasurers to post surety bonds in an amount the Corporation deems sufficient. Restrictions against misleading advertisements are in place, as are fines and jail sentences for violators of the statute. The District of Columbia has no laws regulating recruiting agents of degree-granting institutions. The statutes specifically prohibit institutions from implying in their titles any official connections with the United States government or the District of Columbia government. This prohibition is also applicable to nonresidents and foreign corporations conferring degrees in the District of Columbia. (Relatively Strong Statutes)

John G. Stone, III
Executive Director
Educational Institution Licensure Commission
Suite M-102
605 C Street, NW
Washington, D.C. 20001
(202) 727-3511

Florida

Site visits are required during the period before the State Board of Independent Colleges and Universities considers the application and during a period of temporary licensure (authorization). All out-of-state institutions except those with a religious exemption are regulated on the same basis as in-state institutions. Authorization and exemptions are reviewed annually. Misleading advertisements are specifically prohibited. Recruiting agents are regulated. The Board maintains an up-to-date list of authorized institutions. The state's penalty statute was strengthened in 1986 to include probation and fines in addition to misdemeanor charges. A relatively large number of institutions and categories of institutions are exempt from the authorization requirements (e.g., chartered religious colleges). A grandfather clause also exempts Florida colleges "the credits or degrees of which are accepted for credit by at least three accredited colleges of higher learning, which were exempt prior to July 1, 1982." Florida's current statutes are a vast improvement over earlier laws that encouraged the establishment of a number of very questionable institutions in the state. (Average Strength Statutes)

C. Wayne Freeberg (Dr.)
Executive Director
State Board of Independent Colleges and Universities

Mailing Address:
c/o Department of Education
Tallahassee, FL 32399
(904) 488-8695

Location:
Suite D-13
Sun Federal Place
345 South Magnolia
Tallahassee, FL 32301
(904) 487-3673

Sandra Lee Knight
Associate Director
State Board of Independent Colleges and Universities

Mailing Address
c/o Department of Education
Tallahassee, FL 32399
(904) 487-3673

Georgia

Georgia requires "such investigation of the applicant as the [State Board of Education] may deem necessary or appropriate." A site visit is required for initial authorization and periodically thereafter as determined by the State Board of Education. Relatively numerous categories of institutions are exempt from the authorization process. Georgia does make violation of its statutes punishable by a $1,000 fine, and requires a surety bond from $5,000 to $50,000, depending on enrollment. Agents of educational institutions are regulated. Amendments to the statutes in 1987 explicitly prohibit the sale of postsecondary degrees, diplomas, or certificates. Use of fraudulent credentials and transcripts in connection with any business, trade, profession, or occupation is also prohibited. (Average Strength Statutes)

Janie W. Smith (Dr.)
Coordinator, Private College and University Standards
Georgia Department of Education
1870 Twin Towers East, Capitol Square
Atlanta, GA 30334
(404) 656-2538

Hawaii

The state has no statutes governing authorization of non-accredited, degree-granting, postsecondary education institutions. As a matter of policy, Hawaii does not respond to inquiries and does not wish to be included in this survey. (Relatively Weak Statutes)

Idaho

The state government plays no significant role in evaluating the financial stability or degree program quality of its educational institutions. Educational institutions must, however, register with the Department of Education and post a $10,000 surety bond. Registered (authorized) institutions must refrain from use of terms such as "accredited," "approved," or "licensed" in advertising. Only "registered" is acceptable in such ads. Any agent selling courses must have an agent's permit. Both registered institutions and their agents must reapply for registration annually. A relatively higher number of categories of institutions are exempt from regulation. Idaho makes violations of the statutes punishable by a $1,000 fine or a six-month sentence. (Relatively Weak Statutes)

Eldon Nelson
Supervisor of Support Services
Idaho State Department of Education
Len B. Jordon Office Building
650 West State Street
Boise, ID 83720
(208) 334-2206

Illinois

A two-step process is required of new institutions wishing to operate and award degrees. The institution must first receive authorization to operate and must within three years thereafter achieve degree-granting authority. An application is reviewed and a site visit conducted for both operating authority and for each degree being considered. If the expertise does not exist on the staff, the Board of Higher Education at its expense obtains the services of an out-of-state consultant to review the application in light of the applicable criteria. Authorization is awarded for specific degrees at specific sites. An annual review process is in place for each authorization granted by the Board. Violation of the statute can result in revocation of authority to operate and/or grant degrees. False, deceptive, misleading, or unfair advertising is prohibited. Catalogs and brochures must contain information describing degree programs offered, program objectives, length of program, schedule of tuition, fees, and all other charges and expenses necessary for completion of the courses of study. This and related information must be available to students prior to their enrollment. A surety bond is not required. There is no exemption from statutory regulation for degree-granting religious institutions. (Relatively Strong Statutes)

Kathleer. Kelly (Dr.)
Associate Director for Academic and Health Affairs
Illinois Board of Higher Education
500 Reisch Building
4 West Old Capitol Square
Springfield, IL 62701
(217) 782-3442

Indiana

A four-step process to "accreditation" (authorization) is specified. On-site visits, including consulting experts when needed, are required in order to verify the quality of an organization's facilities and programs. Restrictions against possible abuses by agents of educational organizations are in place, as are restrictions against false advertising. A surety bond ($50,000 maximum) is required for authorization. Authorization must be renewed every five years. Most violations of the statute are considered as misdemeanors. A person who, with intent to defraud, represents himself or herself to be an agent of a postsecondary proprietary educational institution commits a felony. Certain religious institutions are exempt from regulation. Out-of-state institutions, however, are not exempt. (Note: The proprietary nomenclature in the name of the Commission is misleading with reference to the broad scope of the agency's mission.) (Relatively Strong Statutes)

Phillip H. Roush
Commissioner
Indiana Commission on Proprietary Education
32 East Washington St.
Suite 804
Indianapolis, IN 46204
(317) 232-1320

Iowa

Iowa does not require on-site visits for registration (authorization) of educational institutions. Institutions must renew such registration annually. A relatively large number of categories of institutions are exempt from the registration process. No civil or criminal penalties are in place against violators of the state's statutes. Iowa does have restrictions against false advertisements, and the state requires a $50,000 surety bond. While Iowa's statutes covering higher education are relatively weak, the state does have a very strong consumer protection law which applies to higher education as well as to other areas. (Relatively Weak Statutes)

(C) Robert J. Barak (Dr.)
Director of Academic Affairs and Research
State Board of Regents
Lucas State Office Building
Des Moines, IA 50319
(515) 281-3934

Kansas

Approved institutions must meet the standards of the Kansas State Board of Regents before approval (authorization); accreditation by an agency recognized by the Board of Regents satisfies that requirement. Site visits are required by a "committee of higher education peers" before authorization can be attained. This process must be repeated every ten years. A surety bond ($20,000 minimum) is required. There are no restrictions on advertising. (Average Strength Statutes)

Martine Hammond (Dr.)
Director of Academic Affairs
Kansas Board of Regents
14th Floor, Merchants National Bank
Topeka, KS 66612
(913) 296-3421

Kentucky

The Council on Higher Education in Kentucky requires that educational institutions establish financial stability and program quality when applying for licensure or license (authorization) renewal. Site visits may be conducted during the licensing process, and expert consultants are required. A surety bond of $5,000–$50,000, based on enrollment, is required. Advertisements are reviewed during the authorization process. There are no restrictions on the activities of an institution's agents and no penalties for violations of the authorization statutes. Proprietary institutions (including those offering associate degrees) are regulated by the Kentucky State Board for Proprietary Education. However, should such an institution seek to award degrees at the baccalaureate or higher levels, it would be subject to the jurisdiction of the Kentucky Council on Higher Education. (Average Strength Statutes)

Aphrodite Brough (Dr.)
Associate Director for Academic Program
Kentucky Council on Higher Education
1050 U.S. 127 South
Frankfort, KY 40601
(502) 564-3553

Robert Summers
Executive Director
Kentucky State Board for Proprietary Education
P.O. Box 456
Frankfort, KY 40602
(502) 564-4233

Louisiana

Louisiana requires educational institutions only to register (or incorporate), a process that does not constitute approval by the state. Such registration is renewed annually. No higher level of state authorization is available. The state statute poses requirements that are so minimal there is no obvious reason for an institution to operate in violation of them. (Relatively Weak Statutes)

Larry Tremblay (Dr.)
Coordinator of Research and Data Analysis
Louisiana Board of Regents
161 Riverside Mall
Baton Rouge, LA 70801
(504) 342-4253

Maine

Any postsecondary education institution seeking to award a degree must obtain legislative authorization through a "private and special law." Authorization is granted for specific degrees. On-site reviews of the institution are conducted during the authorization process to ensure financial stability and degree quality and are conducted by a team consisting of individuals from other Maine postsecondary education institutions. This team must be approved by the State Board of Education. Following the visit, the team makes a report and recommendation for action to the Board and the legislature. No surety bonding is required but there are some restrictions on advertising prior to authorization being granted. Violations of Maine's statutes are punishable by a $5,000 fine. (Relatively Strong Statutes)

Frederick Douglas
Director
Higher Education Services
State Department of Education and Cultural Services
State Department of Education Building
Augusta, ME 04333
(207) 289-5800

Maryland

Maryland requires on-site visits for authorization of an educational institution, for renewal of that authorization, and for authorization of specific degree programs. On-site visits are designed to ensure that the institution's administration, faculty, curriculum, facilities, library, and publications comply with minimum requirements set by the State Board of Higher Education. Maryland requires a $500,000 surety bond before authorizing a four-year college and a $300,000 surety bond before authorizing an associate-level college. Religious colleges may be exempted if they can certify that their programs are purely religious and that they are financially stable. (Relatively Strong Statutes)

Donald Stoddard (Dr.)
Coordinator, Academic Affairs
State Board for Higher Education
16 Francis Street
Annapolis, MD 21401
(301) 974-2971

Massachusetts

Higher education institutions in Massachusetts are reviewed every twelve years, and proprietary (for-profit) organizations are reviewed every three years. A visiting committee may be appointed to perform on-site evaluations. Authorization is required for specific degree programs. A consumer protection clause protects the consumer against misleading advertisements. Out-of-state institutions must apply for degree granting authorization. No institutions are exempt from authorization statutes. (Relatively Strong Statutes)

John Weston (Dr.)
Academic Program Officer
Division of Academic Affairs
Massachusetts Board of Regents of Higher Education
One Ashburton Place, Room 1401
Boston, MA 02108
(617) 727-7785

Michigan

An on-site visit is required in Michigan before an educational institution is authorized to operate, and a site visit is required before a change in an academic program is authorized. Annual reports to the State Board of Education are required. However, a legal requirement for triennial inspection has not been implemented. No institutions are exempted from authorization statutes. (Average Strength Statutes)

David Hanson
Specialist, Accreditation and Approval
State Department of Education
P.O. Box 30008
Lansing, MI 48909
(517) 373-6551

Minnesota

In Minnesota a site visit to verify information for approval (authorization) of educational institutions is optional. Information submitted by educational institutions for registration is used to determine approval. No restrictions are placed on agents of educational institutions except that they must identify themselves properly. Penalties are not listed for violations of the statute. Minnesota requires degree programs and courses to register yearly and requires institutions that have no binding agreement preserving student records to post a $20,000 surety bond. Restrictions against misleading advertisements are listed. Certain religious institutions are exempt from statutory regulations. (Average Strength Statutes)

E. Ann Kelly (Dr.)
Manager of Programs
Minnesota Higher Education Coordinating Board
Suite 400, Capitol Square Building
550 Cedar Street
Saint Paul, MN 55101
(612) 296-9699

Mississippi

Mississippi's Commission on College Accreditation has authority to "accredit" (authorize) postsecondary educational institutions that wish to operate in Mississippi. The Commission has adopted the standards of the Southern Association of Colleges and Schools and requires full accreditation from that organization before an institution can qualify for full "accreditation" by Mississippi's Commission. Educational institutions have seven years to reach full "accreditation" from the state. Institutions must reach "candidate" status by the fifth year, and they are subject to a site visit if one is deemed appropriate and necessary. Bible colleges in Mississippi must show they have applicant status, provisional accreditation, and eventual full accreditation from the American Association of Bible Colleges. Theological seminaries must show similar recognition from the Association of Theological Schools. Provisionally approved institutions are required to submit annual reports and receive annual approval. Court action is required to remove authorization to award degrees and to remove an institution's name from the annual list of "approved" institutions. The only restriction on advertising applies to institutions not holding full "accreditation" from the state. Some institutions continue to operate and award degrees under a "grandfather clause" enacted in 1964. (Average Strength Statutes)

George Carter
Executive Secretary
Board of Trustees of State Institutions of Higher
    Learning
P.O. Box 2336
Jackson, MS 39205
(601) 982-6611

Missouri

Proprietary institutions may be authorized to operate and award degrees without any state-sponsored review of program quality. The Coordinating Board for Higher Education Board may, however, investigate applicants. Missouri also examines for consumer fraud protection. By "proprietary school," Missouri means "any person not specifically exempted . . . which offers or maintains on either a profit or not for profit basis . . . a course or courses of instruction or study through classroom instruction or correspondence." Certificates of approval (authorization) are required before courses may be offered or degrees awarded. The board may require posting of a "security bond" of not less than $5,000 or 10 percent of the preceding year's gross tuition but may not exceed $25,000. A seven-member Proprietary School Advisory Committee is appointed by the Board; members must be either individual proprietors, general partners of partnerships, or managerial employees of proprietary schools. Missouri exempts a relatively large number of institutions from regulation under its statutes including: (1) religious, denominational, or charitable organizations exempt from property taxation, and (2) any college or university represented directly or indirectly on the Coordinating Board's Advisory Committee. It is relatively easy for an organization to qualify for the religious exemption. The Board may dispense with investigation of out-of-state applicants and grant authorization if it finds the applicant is authorized in another state with statutes roughly equivalent to Missouri's. Violations of the statutes are considered as misdemeanors and are punishable under Missouri law. (Relatively Weak Statutes)

> Robert Jacob (Dr.)
> Assistant Commissioner
> Department of Higher Education
> 101 Adams Street
> Jefferson City, MO 65101
> (314) 751-2361

Montana

Licensing (authorization) of educational institutions by the state is required, but the state has no significant role in evaluating the institution's financial stability or program quality. No site visit is required. However, the Department of Commerce may request further information and conduct any investigation it believes to be appropriate. Montana does place restrictions on misleading advertisements and on the activities of agents of educational institutions. Penalties are established for violations of the statutes. Annual renewal of authorization requires submission of financial statements including balance sheet and curriculum changes. Surety bonds ($10,000 for institutions and $1,000 for agents) are required and must be renewed annually. No degree-granting institutions are exempted from these requirements. (Relatively Weak Statutes)

> (C) Carrol Krause
> Commissioner for Higher Education
> Montana University System
> 33 South Last Chance Gulch
> Helena, MT 59620
> (406) 444-6570

Nebraska

"Provisional accreditation" (authorization) of nonaccredited schools for three years is allowed and is renewable for another three years without an explicit site visit requirement. Some out-of-state institutions are exempted from state requirements but no in-state institutions are so exempted. (Relatively Weak Statutes)

Sue Gordon-Gessner
Executive Director
Nebraska Coordinating Commissioner for
Postsecondary Education
P.O. Box 95005
301 Centennial Mall South
Lincoln, NE 68509
(402) 471-2847

Nevada

"Licensing" (authorization) requires on-site visits by a panel that may include representatives of businesses or institutions affected by the educational organization and individuals with special knowledge of the field. Specific degree programs must be authorized, with investigation, if necessary. Comprehensive prohibitions against misleading advertising are enacted. A $5,000 surety bond is required for authorization. Activities of agents for both in-state and out-of-state educational institutions are regulated. Authorization must be renewed every two years and is usually completed administratively. However, each new program or degree to be offered must be separately approved by the Commission on Postsecondary Education. (Relatively Strong Statutes)

John V. Griffin
Administrator
Nevada Commission on Postsecondary Education
State Capitol Complex
1000 East William, Suite 102
Carson City, NV 89710
(702) 885-5690

New Hampshire

The Postsecondary Education Commission is charged with authorizing both in-state and out-of-state institutions to op-

erate and grant specific degrees for a stated period of years.
The statutes say that on-site inspections of educational institutions are to be conducted by the Commission "where possible" In practice, such inspections are accomplished for all
nonaccredited institutions seeking degree-granting authority.
Renewal of authorization requires a "reevaluation," but not
a site visit. Each proposed new degree program must be submitted to the Commission for prior evaluation and approval.
Anyone violating the statute regarding degree-granting authority in New Hampshire is guilty of a misdemeanor if a
person or a felony if a corporation. In addition, the Commission has authority to seek injunctive relief in situations involving educational institutions. (Average Strength Statutes)

James A. Busselle (Dr.)
Executive Director
Postsecondary Education Commission
2 ½ Beacon Street
Concord, NH 03301
(603) 271-2555

New Jersey

Educational corporations in New Jersey must obtain licensure (authorization) from the Board of Higher Education,
and must obtain approval for any course of study leading to
a degree. Financial stability must be established, either by
the State of New Jersey auditor or by an annual audit by an
independent CPA. Program quality is required in such areas
as the educational program, faculty, library, student services,
physical facilities, and publications. The Department of Higher
Education employs external consultants to assist it in the
evaluation of authorization petitions for new degree programs. Authorization may be granted for a period not to exceed five years. The New Jersey Licensure and Approval
Advisory Board makes recommendations to the Chancellor
and to the Board of Higher Education on applications for
licensure by nonaccredited New Jersey institutions and all
out-of-state institutions. Proprietary institutions in New Jer-

sey may be licensed to grant the associate in applied science degree for up to five years before renewing their application. (Relatively Strong Statutes)

Amorita Suarez
Director
Office of Program Review, Accreditation and Licensure
Department of Higher Education
225 West State Street
Trenton, NJ 08625
(609) 292-2955

New Mexico

New Mexico grants educational institutions a "certificate of *approval*" after two years of operation. Thereafter, annual renewal is required. The state, however, does not actually "approve" the institution, it simply registers it. Although a "survey" of the institution is required by the Commission on Higher Education, no significant role is played by the state in the authorization process. New Mexico offers exemption to its statutes to a relatively large number of different categories of educational institutions (e.g., nonprofit religious institutions). Agents are required to pay a $5.00 fee. A $5,000 surety bond is required of institutions, and misleading ads are restricted. Violations of the statutes may be punished by a $1,000 fine or imprisonment for not more than six months, or both. An attempt to strengthen these statutes failed in the 1987 legislative session. New Mexico's Commission on Higher Education has recently been given oversight responsible for all "proprietary" institutions—a term statutorily defined as including *both* for-profit and not-for-profit organizations. (Relatively Weak Statutes)

(C) Rosalie A. Bindel (Dr.)
Associate Executive Director for Academic Affairs
Commission on Higher Education
1068 Cerrillos Road
Santa Fe, NM 87501-4295
(505) 827-8300

New York

Institutions are chartered by the Regents of The University of the State of New York and receive specific authority in their charter to confer degrees. Site visits are made by State Education Department personnel and consultants expert in the subject fields being reviewed to ensure the quality of postsecondary level educational facilities and programs (including off campus offerings). Organizations may qualify for provisional or absolute charters. The Board of Regents has delegated to the Commissioner of Education the responsibility for registering (authorizing) all degree and certificate programs including those out-of-state institutions. New York regulates the actions of agents of educational institutions and prohibits misleading advertisements. Penalties for violation of state statutes are listed. (Relatively Strong Statutes)

Denis F. Paul (Dr.)
Assistant Commissioner for Higher
Education Academic Review
New York State Education Department
Cultural Education Center—Room 5A37
Empire State Plaza
Albany, NY 12330
(518) 474-8299

Kevin Reilly (Dr.)
Director, Division of Academic Program Review
New York State Education Department
Cultural Education Center—Room 5A37
Empire State Plaza
Albany, NY 12330
(518) 474-3871

North Carolina

The North Carolina rules and standards relating to state oversight of postsecondary education are, to a significant extent, based on the "Model Licensing Law" developed in 1973 by the Education Commission of the States. On-site review of nonaccredited educational institutions that "may necessi-

tate use of a team of examinees" is required before an institution can be licensed (authorized). A surety bond of at least
$10,000 is required. No person or agency with whom an au-
thorized institution contracts is to have a record of unprofes-
sional conduct or incompetence that would reasonably call into
question the overall quality of the institution. False, deceptive, misleading, or unfair practices associated with promotion, sales, collection, or credit are prohibited. Exempt from
authorization requirements (including oversight under the most
recent statutes) are institutions continuously conducting postsecondary degree activity in North Carolina since July 1, 1972;
certain types of religious institutions; and institutions conducting postsecondary education degree activity within the
military. State statutes are published in an unusually well-
designed and clearly written catalogue. (Average Strength
Statutes)

John F. Corey (Dr.)
Associate Vice President for Planning
The University of North Carolina, General
    Administration
P.O. Box 2688
Chapel Hill, NC 27514
(919) 962-6981

North Dakota

All postsecondary educational institutions must be ac-
credited by an agency recognized by the U.S. Department of
Education. The Board of Higher Education may require ad-
ditional evidence and make further investigation if necessary.
Institutions seeking their first authorization to operate may
be provisionally authorized on an annual basis until accredited.
Full authorization is withheld until accreditation is achieved.
(Average Strength Statutes)

Ellen Chaffee (Dr.)
Associate Commissioner for Academic Affairs
State Board of Higher Education
State Capitol Building

Bismarck, ND 58505
(701) 224-2960

Ohio

Nonprofit educational institutions seeking a certificate of authorization in Ohio must be initially authorized and periodically reauthorized by the Board of Regents for each degree program offered. This authorization is both time and site specific for each program. Institutions seeking "certification," (authorization) may be, and usually are, examined on site by representatives of the Board of Regents. The representatives (usually Regents' staff and external consultants) have the right to inspect school records as well as Regents' records. The Board of Regents may require that the award of general degrees be limited to specific areas of instruction until such time as an institution can demonstrate that appropriate resources for instruction have been developed. The conduct of out-of-state institutions is covered thoroughly by Ohio's statutes. Action may be taken against misleading advertising.

Note: Proprietary (for-profit) institutions offering postsecondary degree instruction in Ohio are subject to the authority of the Ohio Board of School and College Registration rather than to the authority of the Ohio Board of Regents. All organizations, firms, and partnerships must apply for and receive a certificate of registration (authorization) before they may confer the associate or baccalaureate degree. The certificate is valid for two years. No new programs may be offered until the program has been registered and approved by the Board. A surety bond of $10,000 is required. Out-of-state schools must secure a certificate of registration before soliciting students in Ohio. An agent of any school must apply for and receive an agent's permit before soliciting business. Penalties for violations of the statutes are specified. (Relatively Strong Statutes)

Jonathan Tafel (Dr.)
Director, Certificates of Authorization and Continuing
   Education
Ohio Board of Regents

3600 State Office Tower
30 East Broad Street
Columbus, OH 43215
(614) 466-3334
(Also Ms. Linda Ogden at the same address)

Maurice Jones
Executive Secretary
Ohio State Board of School and College Registration
30 East Broad Street
Columbus, OH 43215
(614) 466-2752

Oklahoma

The Oklahoma State Regents for Higher Education formulate the regulations and standards by which private educational institutions are "accredited" (authorized), unless the institutions are accredited by a regional agency. Private educational institutions in existence prior to the 1981 statute are exempt from its provisions. The Oklahoma Higher Education Code covering private colleges and universities (Article XI, Sections 140–144) is very brief. No explicit provision is made for institutional site visits, surety bonding, false advertising penalties for violations, etc. (Relatively Weak Statutes)

(C) Melvin R. Todd (Dr.)
Vice Chancellor for Academic Administration
Oklahoma State Regents for Higher Education
500 Education Building
State Capitol Complex
Oklahoma City, OK 73105
(405) 521-2444

Oregon

The Oregon Educational Coordinating Commission may send a representative or a committee to inspect and review an educational institution applying for authorization. Authorization may be granted for a term not to exceed five years.

Each degree program must be authorized. Site reviews are conducted for renewal of authorization. Restrictions against misleading advertising are enacted. No nonaccredited institutions are exempted from regulation. Penalties up to $500 may be levied against violators of the statutes. Graduate schools of theology are exempt (for professional degrees in religion). Surety bonding (amount equal to total tuition receipts for a term) may be required if the institution's financial base is considered to be weak. (Relatively Strong Statutes)

David A. Young (Dr.)
Administrator, Academic Degree
Office of Educational Policy and Planning
Oregon Educational Coordinating Commission
225 Winter Street NE
Salem, OR 97310
(503) 378-3921

Pennsylvania

Site visits of proposed educational degree-granting institutions are conducted by teams that include appropriate experts. The organization is required to have $500,000 of unencumbered endowment. Institutions not accredited by a nationally recognized agency are to be evaluated every five years. Additional program and degree approval after the initial request is dependent upon an institution's charter or articles of incorporation. However, since 1969, every new institution must have each new program leading to a degree approved, as well each new degree. Each degree program of an institution is to be audited every five years by the institution. A statement indicating the procedures utilized and the results must be submitted to the Department of Education upon request. All out-of-state institutions must receive authorization to operate. There are penalties for violations of the statutes. (Relatively Strong Statutes)

Warren D. Evans (Dr.)
Chief, Division of Postsecondary Education Services
Acting Chief, Division of Program Approval
Chartering/Governance/Accreditation Specialist

Pennsylvania Department of Education
333 Market Street
Harrisburg, PA 17126-0333
(717) 783-8228

Puerto Rico

No private or out-of-state higher education institution can be established and operated in Puerto Rico without being previously authorized by the Council on Higher Education. Evaluation teams from both accredited nonpublic and the Commonwealth universities are appointed by the Council on Higher Education and are asked to provide advice about governance, financial stability, faculty, curriculum, library, learning resources, physical facilities, and public liability. Renewal of authorization is required every four years for both the institution and its programs of study. Prior approval of any new program is also required. Theological schools granting religious-service degrees not intended to result in eligibility for positions of employment outside of the religion to which they are oriented are exempt from provisions of the authorization statute. (Relatively Strong Statutes)

Ismael Ramirex Soto (Dr.)
Executive Director,
Office of the Council on Higher Education of
    Puerto Rico
Box F
University of Puerto Rico Station
San Juan, Puerto Rico 00931
(809) 758-3350 or 3356

Madeline Quilichini
Associate Director, Licensing and Accreditation
Office of the Council on Higher Education of Puerto
  Rico
Box F
University of Puerto Rico Station
San Juan, Puerto Rico 00931
(809) 758-3350 or 3356

Rhode Island

No institution may grant degrees without obtaining authorization from the Board of Governors for Higher Education. The Board is quite explicit in stating its responsibilities for regulatory intentions governing (1) proprietary schools; (2) in-state institutions of higher education; and (3) out-of-state institutions of higher education. The published protocols of the Board provide for site visits, restrictions on misleading advertising, and penalties for violation of the statutes. Rhode Island has very detailed criteria for use in reviewing proposals submitted by institutions wishing to offer degree programs in the state. (Relatively Strong Statutes)

Cynthia Ward (Dr.)
Associate Commissioner of Program and Planning
Rhode Island Office of Higher Education
199 Promenade Street
Providence, RI 02908
(401) 277-2685

South Carolina

A team site visit to educational institutions seeking authorization is required. The state authorizes specific degree programs and requires accredited institutions from other states to be authorized. A surety bond of at least $10,000 is required. Site visits are not necessarily required for renewal of authorization but in practice are carried out by the Commission on Higher Education. A penalty of as much as $5,000 may be imposed for violations of the statutes. Institutions and their agents are prohibited from engaging in advertising, sales, collection, credit, or other practices which are false, deceptive, misleading, or unfair. Bible schools and theological schools are exempt. (Average Strength Statutes)

Alan S. Krech
Assistant Director for Planning and Special Projects
South Carolina Commission on Higher Education
1429 Senate Street
Columbia, SC 29201
(803) 253-6260

South Dakota

Postsecondary education institutions "wishing to maintain, advertise, solicit for, or conduct a course of instruction in the state" must apply for an institutional license. Applicants for a license must show sound financial condition; must post a surety bond of $10,000 for the institution and (eventually) a $1,000 bond for each agent; and must give evidence of sound educational programs and safe living and studying facilities. No site visit or personal verification of the information submitted is required. Applicants pay a $100 fee; renewal each year costs $50. "An applicant need not resubmit all information required in the initial application at the time of renewal." No site visit is required for renewal. Solicitors, or agents, must pay a fee of $25 (renewed annually for $10) and sign an affidavit stating they have a copy of the statutes and are familiar with them. South Dakota's statute requires that each school's catalogue or brochure contain specific relevant information for students. Institutions and their agents are prohibited from using false advertisements. A relatively large number of categories of institutions are exempt from South Dakota's statutes. (Relatively Weak Statutes)

(C) Roxie Thielen
Administrative Aide
South Dakota Department of Education and
    Cultural Affairs
Richard Kneip Building
700 Governors Drive
Pierre, SD 57501-2293
(605) 773-3134

Tennessee

Tennessee adopted the 1973 "Model Licensing Law" developed by the Education Commission of the States, which gives an agency of authorization the power, among other things, to "receive, investigate, and act upon applications for authorization to operate." Annual reauthorization is required. Each renewal application must include submission of the same information and materials as are required for initial authorization. No specific requirement for site visits is included. The state restricts activities of agents, requires a $10,000 surety bond, and restricts misleading advertising. A civil penalty of $500 per day for each day of violation may be levied. Criminal sanctions may be sought by the state or district attorney. (Relatively Strong Statutes)

George M. Roberts (Dr.)
Director of Licensure/Veterans Education
Tennessee Higher Education Commission
Parkway Towers, Suite 1900
404 James Robertson Parkway
Nashville, TN 37219
(615) 741-3605

Texas

Educational institutions must operate as nondegree-granting institutions or educational or training establishments for at least two years before becoming eligible for certificates of authority to grant degrees. An institution may be "certified" (authorized) for no more than eight years (four two-year certificates) during which time it is expected to become accredited by a recognized accrediting agency and, thereby, exempt from the authorization law. Before certificates are granted, a site visit by experts is required. Violations of the statutes are punishable by fines of $1,000 to $5,000. Certificates of authority are renewed if the Texas Board finds the institution has maintained all standards. Site visits are customary but not required for renewal. The state requires that a list of agents of educational institutions be provided, but does not require additional regulation. In transmitting a certificate of authority, the Coordinating Board of the Texas College and University System specifies the exact language that must be used whenever reference is made to the certificate in publications, advertisements, or any other representations. Such language includes a disclaimer that the certificate does *not* constitute accreditation, but only that the institution has met the Board's minimum standards established for purposes of consumer protection. (Relatively Strong Statutes)

David T. Kelley (Dr.)
Director of Institutional Certification
Texas Higher Education Coordinating Board
University and Health Affairs
P.O. Box 12780, Capitol Station
Austin, TX 78711
(512) 462-6491

Utah

Both educational institutions and their agents are required to register with the State Board of Regents every two years. Upon satisfactory completion of a comprehensive application, either a certificate of authority or a permit is awarded. The necessity of a site visit is predicated upon need. No surety bond is required. A relatively large number of categories of institutions are exempted from registration. The state neither endorses nor approves the institutions so registered but seeks to elicit as much information about the institution as is "legally advisable." The statutes prohibit false and misleading advertising and provide for full disclosure and specific penalties for violations. (Relatively Weak Statutes)

(C) Sterling R. Provost (Dr.)
Assistant Commissioner for Veterans Education and
    Proprietary Schools
Utah System of Higher Education
355 West North Temple
#3 Triad Center, Suite 550
Salt Lake City, UT 84180-1205
(801) 538-5247

Vermont

An institution must first "register" (incorporate) and state its intentions to operate and offer postsecondary education programs. The next step, which may not take place until the institution has been in existence for eighteen months, is to apply for a certificate of approval or a certificate of degree-granting authority or both. A certificate of approval authorizes the institutions to exist but not to grant degrees. It is intended for use by institutions whose missions do not incorporate degree programs or institutions that do not wish to award degrees until they can secure accreditation. A certificate of degree-granting authority authorizes the institutions to begin awarding degrees. Certificates may be issued for a term not to exceed five years at which time they must be renewed. Either type of "certification" (authorization) involves the submission of a self-study report, a site visit by an evaluation team, and a recommendation to the Vermont Higher Education Council's Committee on Accreditation and Certification based on the team's written report. Issues of financial stability and quality are central to this evaluation process. Violations of the statutes are punishable by a fine not to exceed $1,000, imprisonment for not more than one year, or both. (Relatively Strong Statutes)

> Ann Turkle
> Executive Director
> Vermont Higher Education Council
> Box 70
> Hyde Park, VT 05655
> (802) 888-7771
>
> Sandra Robinson
> Chief of Adult Education Unit
> Vermont Department of Education
> State Office Building
> Montpelier, VT 05602-2703
> (802) 828-3131

Virginia

The Virginia Council of Higher Education must give approval (authorization) for all course work for degree credit and degree programs. Institutions that offer only religious/theological education are exempt under provisions that have at least the potential to permit questionable organizations to escape state oversight. Also exempt are institutions that enroll only active duty military personnel on military bases. All other institutions must demonstrate compliance with authorization standards, as verified by site visit, prior to receiving approval to confer degrees. In-state private institutions receive provisional approval until accreditation is received from a recognized agency deemed appropriate by the council. Out-of-state institutions receive five-year renewable terms of approval for each program at each site and must be fully accredited prior to applying to operate in Virginia. The Council's regulations require specific wording and content in all advertising. The Council may suspend or revoke authorization for violation of its regulations, noncompliance with its standards, or loss of accreditation. Violations of the regulations carry civil and criminal penalties. New administrative regulations adopted in June 1987 specify that instruction via telecommunications requires authorization if offered on an organized schedule at a Virginia site. The new standards also impose specific curriculum and faculty requirements tied to the degree level of an institution's instructional programs. (Average Strength Statutes)

John Molnar (Dr.)
Library Planning and Institutional Approval
Coordinator
State Council of Higher Education for Virginia
James Monroe Building, 9th Floor
101 North 14th Street
Richmond, VA 23219
(804) 225-2634

Washington

Preoperation review using minimum criteria is specified before an institution can be authorized. A site visit is included, and the finances of the institution are also reviewed. Annual reauthorization is required. Restrictions apply to misleading advertising. Out-of-state institutions are regulated under the same statutes applying to domestic institutions. Penalties for violations are explicitly listed. Certain religious institutions are exempt from regulation. Regulation does apply to the secular programs of institutions offering both religious and secular programs. Surety bonds or other security for new institutions is $5,000. Thereafter the amount of the surety bond or security is set at 10 percent of the preceding year's total tuition and fee charges, but not less than $5,000 nor more than $100,000. (Relatively Strong Statutes)

> Elaine Jones
> Policy Associate
> Washington State Council for Postsecondary Education
> 908 East Fifth Avenue
> Olympia, WA 98504
> (206) 753-3241

West Virginia

A site visit by experts is required before an educational institution is authorized for a period of one to four years. A site visit is also required for renewal. Agents of institutions are regulated, and a $50 fee and $1,000 surety bond are required of them. Institutions must post a $20,000 surety bond as well. Misleading advertisements are prohibited, and there are penalties for violations of the statutes. No institutions are exempt from state regulation. (Relatively Strong Statutes)

> Douglas Call (Dr.)
> Director of Community Colleges and
>   Vocational Education
> West Virginia Board of Regents
> 950 Kanawha Boulevard, East
> Charleston, WV 25301
> (304) 348-2101

Wisconsin

All Wisconsin proprietary (for profit) institutions must be examined and "approved" (authorized) by Wisconsin's Educational Approval Board before operating. On-site inspections are part of the authorization process, and authorizations must be renewed annually. An entire chapter of the Board's rules is devoted to regulation of advertising practices. Wisconsin requires an institutional surety bond of $25,000 or more and a $1,000 bond from agents. A $500 fine and three months of imprisonment are specified for soliciting without a permit or for operating an unauthorized school. These statutes and regulations do *not* apply, however, to institutions organized on a nonprofit basis as defined by the U.S. Internal Revenue Code or institutions of a "parochial or denominational character offering courses having a sectarian objective." These categories of institutions are not subject to regulation by the Educational Approval Board or any other Wisconsin state agency. (Relatively Strong Statutes for Proprietary Institutions, Relatively Weak Statutes for Nonaccredited Tax-exempt Private Institutions)

(C) David R. Stucki
Executive Secretary
State of Wisconsin Educational Approval Board
P.O. Box 7874
Madison, WI 53707
(608) 266-1996

Wyoming

Wyoming requires licensing (authorization) of for-profit and nonprofit educational institutions, but requires no site visit or detailed evaluation of program quality. Schools must post a $10,000 performance bond, and agents must pay a $25 fee. Misleading advertising is prohibited. Renewal of authorization requires a $50 fee, but no site visit. Violators are guilty of a misdemeanor and on conviction may be punished by a fine of not more than $100 or by imprisonment for not more than six months, or by both fine and imprisonment. Each solicitation of enrollment or each transaction of business without authorization constitutes a separate offense. (Relatively Weak Statutes)

(C) Lyall Hartley
Director, Certification/Licensure Unit
Wyoming Department of Education
Hathaway Building
Cheyenne, WY 82002
(307) 777-7295

Index

Approval (*continued*)
 degree-granting, 128, 129
 Veterans' benefits, 128, 129
Arizona, 40, 67–68, 70, 133, 134,
 185
 questionable doctoral degrees,
 5–6
 summary of statutes, 210
Arizona Republic (Phoenix), 134
Arkansas, 133
 summary of statutes, 211
Associate degrees, 99–101
Association for Continuing Higher
 Education, 135–136, 182, 185
Association of Advanced
 Rabbinical and Talmudic
 Schools, Accrediting
 Commission, 156
Association of American Colleges,
 102
Association of American Medical
 Colleges, 162
Association of Independent
 California Colleges and
 Universities, 144–145
Association of Independent
 Colleges and Schools,
 Accrediting Commission, 120
Atwell, Robert H., xi
Austria, 174
Authorization, 33, 128, 129, 171
 California Education Code,
 degrees in theology, 147–
 148
 California Education Code,
 Section 94310.3, 146–147
 state governmental, 118

B

Baccalaureate degrees. *See*
 Bachelor's degrees
Bachelor's degrees, 101–103
Bailes, James O., 84
Baylor University Medical Center,
 84
Belgium, 71, 123
Benkin, Ellen, 105
Binker, Barbara, xii
Blevins, Norman W., 91
Board of Governors Bachelor of

Arts Degree Program
 (Illinois), 58
Bob Jones University, 125
Bonker, Don, 74, 76
Bouchard, Odette, 81, 88(p), 89(p)
Brown, Jonathan, xii, 144–145
Buckley Amendment, Family
 Rights and Privacy Act of
 1974, 164
Business, questionable degrees in,
 15

C

Caffey, James, 66–70
California Committee of Bar
 Examiners, 144
California, 17, 24, 40, 48–51, 139–
 151, 185
 Business and Professions Code,
 17
 categories of institutional
 designation, 14
 Council for Private
 Postsecondary Educational
 Institutions, 15
 Department of Education,
 Private Postsecondary
 Education Division, 135,
 140, 141, 143, 144, 145–146,
 147, 149, 176
 Education Code, Section
 94310(b), 140
 Education Code, Section
 94310(c), 140
 foreign operations by authorized
 organizations, 176
 number of approved institutions,
 151
 number of authorized
 institutions, 150–151
 regulation of out-of-state degree
 programs, 119
 summary of statutes, 211–213
Canada, 136
 expert witness, 5
 university applicants from
 California, 4
Cann, Denise, 87(p)
"Capital Institute of Advanced
 Education," 75, 121–122

Carbone, Robert, xii
Caribbean medical schools, 26
Catalogs/promotional literature,
29–31
Center for Adult Learning and
Educational Credentials. *See*
American Council on
Education
Certification, 128, 129–130, 168,
171
CETEC, 81, 84, 88(p), 89(p)
Charles, Prince of Wales, 178
Charter Oak College/Board for
State Academic Awards
(Connecticut), 58
Chartering, 128, 171
Chicago, 71
CIFAS, 81
Clarion-Ledger (Jackson,
Mississippi), 134
Clark, Joseph A., 136
Classification, 128
Cobb, Barry L., xii
College Board, 56
College-Level Examination
Program, 32
Colombia, 178–179
Colorado, summary of statutes,
213
Commission on Higher Education
and the Adult Learner, 56
Competency-based curricula, 54–55
Conclusions, recommendations for
change, 181–192
Connecticut, 133
summary of statutes, 213–214
Consequences of diploma mill
activity, 21–22
Contract learning, 54
Correspondence instruction, 55–56,
57–58, 120
Council for Adult and Experiential
Learning, 32
Council of Europe, 177–178
Council of Graduate Schools in the
United States, 57, 103
Council on Postsecondary
Accreditation, 2, 4, 6, 23–24,
26, 33, 104, 110, 111, 117–119,
122–124
importance of recognition by,
118

organization of, 117
provisions for recognition, 123–
124
U.S. Department of Education
comparison, 155–157
Counseling
businesses, 165–166
questionable degrees in, 15–16
Credential-counsciousness, 12
Credential fraud
control of, 92–95
federal employees, 95
state control of, 94
Credentialing educational
accomplishment,
recommendations on, 105–107
Credentials, fraudulent, 91–92
Credit by examination, 53–54
Credit hours, defined, 98–99
"Cromwell University," 71
Curtis, Mark H., 102
Cyr, David, 87(p)

D

Daniels, Anthony, E., 65–66
Degree-holders (legitimate),
number of, 12
Degrees, 97–108
academic assumptions about, 97–
99
academic, 97–107
backdating, 68
honorary, 29
requirements, 30
titles, 30
Delaware, summary of statutes,
214
de Mesones, Pedro, 26, 80–84,
86(p)
DePaul University, 71
"DePaul University," 71
Diploma mill degrees, how to
identify, 190–191
Diploma mills
addresses, 27
causes of boom, 11–13
characteristics of, 23–34
clients of, 14–15
definition, 9–10